T0166727

VEGAN LIVING

VEGAN LIVING

A simple guide to a cruelty-free,

healthy, plant-based life

ONDINE SHERMAN

LOST
THE
PLOT

LOST
THE
PLOT

A Lost the Plot book, first published in 2020 by Pantera Press Pty Limited
www.PanteraPress.com

A Cataloguing-in-Publication entry for this book is available from the National Library of Australia.

ISBN 978-1-925700-63-3 (Paperback)

Cover, illustrations and internal design: Elysia Clapin
Publisher: Martin Green
Project Editor: Anne Reilly
Editor: Alexandra Payne
Proofreaders: Anna Blackie and Lucy Bell
Printed and bound in China by Shenzhen Jinhao Colour Printing

For my parents, Brian and Gene Sherman.

CONTENTS

FOREWORD

BY JESS AND STEF DADON, FOUNDERS OF HOW TWO LIVE
& ANIMAL-FRIENDLY FOOTWEAR COMPANY TWOOBS

We created our footwear label TWOOBS in 2012 as a fashion-forward animal-friendly alternative to what was on the market. It's been incredible to watch animal welfare finally receive the platform it deserves over the last few years, and with the rise of veganism people are waking up to the fact that we need to be eating and buying more ethically. Recently, key players in the fashion industry have really stepped up to the plate, with brands like Stella McCartney and ASOS leading the change.

In this book, Ondine Sherman helps explain why younger generations are demanding ethical lifestyle choices and why it's so important for us all to lean in to this shift.

For anyone with questions about the vegan lifestyle, Ondine provides honest and relatable information, and shows us that we all have the ability to go on this incredibly rewarding journey.

1

THE TIME IS NOW

'There is nothing so powerful in the world as an idea whose time has come and animal protection is just such an idea.'[1]

THE HONORABLE MICHAEL KIRBY AC CMG

AUSTRALIA'S LONGEST SERVING JUDGE

Yippee! You've taken the first step on the path to a vegan, cruelty-free, plant-based lifestyle and I'm delighted you're here.

If you're an omnivore, pescatarian, vegetarian or even vegan-curious, this book is written just for you. A healthy, happy vegan lifestyle is a win–win–win–win–(repeat infinite times) for you, animals, the environment and the future of our planet.

What's the best time to begin my journey? I hear you ask. How about, now?! You'll be in great company. Animal protection is the social justice movement of our century and the vegan awakening is happening, making history in our very generation. It's worldwide and spontaneous, and involves millions of people shifting away from animal products.

We have a global population of 7.7 billion and, in recent years, 70 per cent of the world's people have reported either reducing or stopping their meat consumption. This has been largely led by millennials concerned about animal protection and the environment.

If you're thinking the vegan movement is populated by only hippies and hipsters, you couldn't be more wrong. Mainstream businesses, multinational corporations and investors are taking note. There's an explosion of new plant-based products, vegan food technology, ethical fashion and, most importantly, passion.

Hundreds of new cookbooks are filling bookstores and celebrity chefs are jumping on board. The world's largest multinationals, renowned for their meat and dairy products, are now investing in vegan food technology. And companies like Google, Burger King and McDonald's are getting on the meat-free train.

Billionaires such as Bill Gates, Jay-Z and Richard Branson are investing heavily in the area while vegan and vegetarian celebrities are influencing their billions of fans. Ariana Grande believes veganism can make you live longer and be happier, Ellen DeGeneres is encouraging her fans to stop eating meat, and Miley Cyrus is sure veganism is taking over the world. Music sensation Billie Eilish told her fans, 'I understand that meat tastes good ... and I know you think you're just one person and it won't change anything if you stop but ... you should know "one person" adds up.'

Harry Bolman, vegan of 39 years, shares the current enthusiasm for veganism:

'The amount of vegan resources, awareness, support and products available today make going vegan a breeze. When it comes to food, there are vegan options popping up everywhere. There's vegan documentaries, support groups, cooking channels, activists, celebrities, festivals, markets, tours, vegan supermarkets, home-delivered vegan food, vegan politicians, vegan dating sites and many fully vegan, ethical companies. It's so easy to choose compassion over cruelty, to choose life over death.'

So many vegan businesses are flourishing that there are now dedicated companies, books and conferences focused on assisting the expanding vegan niche. These facts all point to the future – a world where veganism is the norm, mainstream, while consuming animal products makes you unusual.

THE AIMS OF

This book is intended to give you the tools you need to:

Understand what's happening to animals, the climate and the environment.

You'll be given scientifically based and up-to-date information on key animal issues, sustainability and the climate crisis so you can feel confident in your decision to go vegan and start a conversation.

Start your vegan journey in the healthiest way possible.

Worried about getting enough iron, protein and calcium? Being vegan can be super healthy – even healthier than other diets. How do we know? Some of the world's leading doctors and scientists are collecting the data and coming to clear conclusions.

THIS BOOK

Handle shade from family, friends and that pesky person at the BBQ.

I know all the criticisms and questions that people may throw your way and I have your back.

Enjoy the journey.

Starting your vegan journey will put you in excellent company and you will be spoilt for choice for inspiration and mentors to guide you. Some of the coolest people in the world (not even kidding) are going vegan: #inspiring.

Take your vegan lifestyle and super-size it into real-world advocacy.

If you're outraged about what's happening to pigs in factory farms, sheep in the live export trade, chinchillas in the fur industry, elephants in circuses, orcas in marine parks, bunnies in cosmetics testing, joeys in the hunting industry – and the list goes on – this book can help you become the voice for the voiceless in the way that suits you and your personality.

To help make sure all the advice in this book is spot on, I enlisted the help of about 200 fellow vegans. I call this wonderful group of interviewees our 'Vegan A-Team' and you'll find many of their thoughts and ideas here. They are vegans from all walks of life – friends, colleagues, contacts and people I didn't even know (but do now!). They kindly shared their lived experiences, useful tips and life-changing inspirations. You'll also find extended profiles of some of our A-Team members so you can get a good sense of their vegan journey.

This book takes you through the journey of becoming vegan. I show you the evidence for why to go vegan; discuss all the fabulous food options; talk about other things a vegan lifestyle can involve (such as fashion and advocacy); show you how supportive and diverse the vegan community is, how to ask for help if you need it and how to talk to friends and family about your vegan choice; and, finally, I look to our future. *Vegan Living* is also full of nutrition tips, ideas for snacks and info to get you started in as healthy a way as possible. But this is not a recipe book. Why? Trust me, you'll thank me later. I'm not the world's best cook – my husband literally begged me to stop making him birthday cakes and I wouldn't know a slow-cooker from a toaster oven. In any case, with vegie recipe books from chefs such as Ottolenghi and Jamie Oliver, and hundreds of awesome vegan cookbooks on the market, you have a lot of shopping left to do. And, hello Google, there are a trillion vegan recipes at your fingertips for every different taste, culture and budget.

At its heart, this book is intended to be your personal ally – a helping hand to guide (not pull) you, a kind voice to support you and ease your fears, and a friend to assist you in avoiding possible pitfalls.

TERMS

Pescetarian: A person who doesn't eat meat but does consume fish, eggs and dairy products. *Pesce* means 'fish' in Italian.

Vegetarian: A person who doesn't eat meat or fish but does consume dairy products and eggs (which is why the term 'lacto-ovo-vegetarian' is sometimes used, eg when ordering a special meal on airplanes). The word 'vegetarian' was first used in 1842.

Vegan: While initially a vegan was defined as a person who consumes no food that comes from animals, today the term also commonly encompasses abstaining from non-food products (such as leather) that derive from animals or any exploitative use of animals.

About me

As a small girl, shy and freckled, I was enticed and enchanted by the world of animals. Like many children, I had a special connection with my first dog, Bronnie, and I fantasised that I could talk to her and commune with all other animals.

When I was 7, Bronnie warming my feet under the dinner table, my grandmother served us tongue, a traditional Eastern European dish, and I had my first lightbulb moment. That tongue was *someone's* tongue, that someone was an animal and I loved animals! Fireworks went off in my little head as I understood that all the food I had been eating – the finger-licking chicken, bolognese sauces, and sausage rolls and meat pies from the tuckshop – were all made from dead animals. I promptly declared to my grandmother, parents and brother that I would stop eating meat. My decision excluded eggs, fish and dairy ... and my leather school shoes. Those next steps would come much later.

It was 1981 and not the best time to be vego in carnivorous Australia. Menus were devoid of vegetarian (let alone vegan) options, and there were certainly no plant-based sausages or burgers at the supermarket. At birthday parties, with nothing to replace the burgers, I squeezed tomato sauce onto empty buns. My resolution was cemented when I became involved in the world of animal activism.

At 11, I stuck a poster on my wall that said: *The chicken in your freezer has more room now than it did when it was alive.* And I wrote a letter to the editor of the newsletter of Animal Liberation, *Outcry,* saying, 'I never knew people could do such rotten things to animals. If I was older I would really give those people a hard time.'

By age 15, I'd given up leather and started protesting. I carried anti-fur placards through Sydney's CBD. During duck-hunting season, I rowed onto wetlands to rescue injured water birds shot by hunters – I held a bird in my hand, blood seeping from her beak, as she died in my arms. I moved on to other forms of activism but, being an introvert, wasn't well suited to confrontations.

As an adult, I realised how activism comes in a plethora of forms, each one powerful and necessary. When combined, they create lasting change. In 2004 I founded an organisation together with my wonderful father, Brian Sherman, with the aims of lifting the 'veil of secrecy' on legalised, institutionalised animal cruelty and creating a kinder, more respectful and compassionate world for animals. We named it Voiceless because animals can't demand, protest, demonstrate or represent themselves in courts of law. As Professor Peter Singer, the philosopher often referred to as the founder of the animal rights movement says, 'We have to speak up on behalf of those who cannot speak for themselves.' Animals do speak, of course. We humans just block our ears, failing to hear their voices, choosing not to learn their languages. Since we began our organisation, my father and I haven't stopped working towards our vision and never will.

My childhood pescatarian diet slowly but progressively morphed into veganism. I learned about the horrors of the dairy industry and gave up milk and cheese. Understanding our wonderful watery world made me pause to think about our fishy friends and how they too are sentient, feel pain and need our protection.

Today I'm not a perfect vegan and don't know if I ever will be. But I'm trying. And – surrounded by a society that has woven animal exploitation into every single aspect of its fabric – that, I believe, is the best anyone can do.

I wrote this book because so many people I meet are curious or confused about animal-cruelty issues, farming methods and vegan health and food. I want to answer their questions but, sadly afflicted with a terrible memory, I often struggle to recall the facts and figures I know. This book is my way of summing up all the information in one place, with all the most current scientific and health research noted and annotated. I hope it helps to answer all your questions and more.

ABOUT VOICELESS

After Voiceless was founded in 2004, it quickly became a leader in animal protection and animal law in Australia.

With a vision of a respectful and compassionate world for animals, Voiceless has worked tirelessly to empower – and render mainstream – the animal protection movement, shine a spotlight on cruel industry practices and advance legal protection for animals.

Today, Voiceless is the home of animal law and animal protection education, developing the crucial skill of critical thinking in young people – our next generation of influencers and decision-makers.

Voiceless's Animal Law Education is a multi-faceted program for law schools and students, engaging lawyers in animal-protection issues in our legal system. Working with high-school educators, Voiceless's Animal Protection Education encourages students to think critically about animal protection by providing teachers with the information and tools to explore the human–animal relationship in our society.

Voiceless's patrons are internationally recognised individuals from the highest levels of science, law, business and the arts who are dedicated to raising awareness of Voiceless's mission. Among them are John M. Coetzee, Dr Jane Goodall DBE, The Hon. Michael Kirby AC CMG, Prof. Charlie Teo AM and Ai Weiwei.

ADIT ROMANO

Adit is co-founder of Freedom Farm Sanctuary, a centre for education, compassion and tolerance for all animals.

HOW I BEGAN

As a mother of three, I have been long interested in the connection between what we eat and our health, how we feel, and the way we live our lives. I was vegetarian for 17 years but, thanks to a video from Gary Yourofsky – *The Most Important Speech You Will Ever Hear* – I found out about the price of dairy and eggs on animals and became vegan in an hour.

MY MOTIVATION

I love animals, but animals weren't my driving force for starting Freedom Farm or becoming a vegan. You don't have to be an animal lover in order to not want to harm animals. I believe in justice and if I see injustice, I want to stop it. My life is dedicated to stopping the injustices we inflict upon animals.

VEGAN FOOD

My kids and husband went into shock when I became vegan. I was always the person responsible for cooking and shopping and I had no will to buy animal products anymore for our fridge. I felt guilty when they wanted cheese and I refused! I quickly learned to become the best vegan cook I could be, studying and practising recipes so I could make a varied, tasty and rich assortment of dishes. Today, my kids love my vegan cooking so much they only want to eat at home and all their friends come to us for meals. We don't miss out on anything: we eat all the dishes we used to love – pies, soups, lasagnes and even cheesecakes – just vegan versions which are, in any case, lighter and healthier.

HOW I TALK TO NON-VEGANS

Veganism is a long road and I believe it's better to be smart, not right. Don't blame people or make them feel guilty; focus on the good and let them see how veganism is a positive experience and choose this life for themselves. Be a good example: calm, friendly, respectful and a good listener.

Start slowly

Veganism is not only about what we eat. It is embedded in every part of life, whether it's food, fashion, activities, interests or ways of understanding the world. Here are the main areas I suggest we concentrate on, particularly early in your vegan journey: eating healthy food, building a supportive network of family and friends, choosing beauty products, and transitioning to a skin- and fur-free wardrobe.

But let's pause for a moment. Each of us has a different character, a unique personality. Going vegan could mean an overnight change for one person, while for another it might take months or years.

The level of vegan 'perfection' we attain is also individual. Perfection is a myth – please don't let the fear of not being the most perfect vegan stop you from trying in the first place.

And don't let anyone tell you how vegan you should become. Although the general rule is no animal products, there is a huge spectrum as to where this takes you.

Vegan A-Team member and personal trainer, Shaun Moss, says:

'If you make a mistake and eat something non-vegan for whatever reason, so what? We all have food addictions and social pressures. Don't beat yourself up; it's not a big deal. Every day just try to learn more and do better. Just be patient with yourself.'

Tim Vasudeva, experienced animal advocate, explains:

'There is a really good phrase I try to keep in mind – "as vegan as possible". You (and your social and work circles) aren't going to get it right 100 per cent of the time, so if you're out there doing your best, there is no need to beat yourself up about it (or anyone else) when something occasionally goes wrong.'

The truth is that even for the most dedicated vegans, perfection is tricky to attain. Animal products are seamlessly integrated (and usually unlabelled) in products we would never imagine. Foods that you wouldn't expect to contain non-vegan ingredients include red wine and beer (fishes' bladders or bone marrow), orange and other fruit juices (fish oil), jam (gelatin), soft drinks (insect derivatives), and white and brown sugar (ground animal bones). And sadly it doesn't stop with food.

Other products that may be non-vegan include paintbrushes and make-up brushes (animal hair), tattoo ink (bone char, animal fat), most condoms (milk derivative), lipstick and mascara (fish scales), crayons (beef tallow), watercolour paint (ox gall) and many more.

For me, it has been a two-steps-forward, one-step-backward process since I was seven years old. These days, being the tortoise I am, I'm still shuffling along my path, getting closer to what I would I see as 'perfect' – for me, that is. Many of my friends and colleagues have experienced something similar.

Kindness is important not only for animals and other people but for yourself too, and I believe the most important thing to remember is this – it's absolutely okay if we stumble along the way, if it takes time. This journey can last a day or a year, or slowly unfold over decades. Be patient. Changing one's diet, clothing and daily habits can have its challenges, but the benefits are worth it.

Even if you are determined to strive for perfection, give yourself a pat on the back for every positive step you take. You know how kids have star charts to help them get into good habits? Adults need that too. Giving yourself credit for small changes will only strengthen your resolve. Venture forth on your vegan journey at the pace right for you. Set small goals along the way as goal-setting is key to any successful behavioural change.

If you're not quite ready to make an immediate change to full-blown veganism, start slowly. Maybe begin with two vegan meals a day or by simply using a plant-based milk instead of cow's milk in your coffee and on your cereal. Remember – going vegan for even one day can save one animal's life. A single year of veganism saves 1022 square metres of forest, 3322 kilograms of CO_2 and 6607 kilograms of grain![2]

To help you begin, start with one of these tried-and-true techniques below to reduce animal products.

1. **Veganuary:** This is one of the most popular ways to give veganism a try and happens during the month of January. Every year the number of participants doubles. In 2020, a record-breaking 400,000 people signed the pledge from every single country in the world except North Korea, Vatican City and Eswatini (formerly known as Swaziland).

2. **Meat Free Mondays:** Tons of workplaces, schools and institutions are getting on board with this worldwide phenomenon, which was first launched by long-time vegetarian Sir Paul McCartney and two of his daughters, Mary and famous fashion designer Stella – both vegan – in 2009. You can try it at home. Log your meat-free days via the inspirational app, The Darwin Challenge, created by Jacqui Courtney and Chris Darwin, the great-great-grandson of Charles Darwin.

3. **Swapping single foods:** The easiest way to start cutting down is to take a single product and replace it with a plant-based alternative – for example, beef for beans on your taco Tuesdays.

4. **Vegan before six/after six:** Basically, swap one or two meals a day with vegan options. Slowly, you'll get a taste of what a vegan lifestyle could be like.

5. **Challenge 22:** Some say that it takes 21 days to create a new habit, so Challenge 22 added an extra day for luck. Try this challenge any time of the year and see how it works. Join the online groups for ideas, tips and support. According to their surveys, 40 per cent of participants went from eating meat to veganism or vegetarianism while another 33 per cent went from vego to vegan.

6. **Reducetarian:** This is a fancy way of saying, 'Hey, it's not all or nothing!' Reduce your consumption of animal products and it will make a significant difference for you, the animals and the environment.

Grace Prael, Vegan A-Team member, talks about how once you start, you never want to go back:

'Eventually, once you have built up a lot of knowledge, heard a lot of faulty counterarguments, successfully gotten through social awkwardness and cooking experiments, read news article after news article about how the market for vegan products is booming while simultaneously seeing articles about how devastating climate change really is, I think you just realise that you never want to go back to your old way of being. It becomes unimaginable to go back. It's a point you can get to and find really fulfilling over time, through informing yourself and committing to positive moral change.'

Most importantly, know that whichever path you take, you will be creating a positive imprint on the world.

2

WHY VEGAN

'There's no pillow as soft as a
clear conscience.'

FRENCH PROVERB

Veganism is a joyful way of life – a conscious, responsible, ethical decision to live without harming, exploiting or killing other sentient beings. It's a life based on the principles of peace and non-violence, and one brimming with kindness, respect and compassion to all living creatures and the Earth.

Don't we all want a world that's more caring, just, fair and less violent? Let's give that a resounding YES!

Vegan living is not hard. Most of us living in industrialised countries have unprecedented choice about what we can eat. Our supermarkets overflow with a wide variety of products and, if we're lucky, with a click of a button, food, fashion and beauty products are delivered directly to our doors. We are able to easily meet our nutritional needs and keep up with style trends without supporting industries known to cause both harm to animals and environmental destruction.

But remember – veganism is not a diet, fad, club, fashion or cult. It isn't a new-age concern at all. For thousands of years, veganism and vegetarianism have been a part of Asian Buddhism, Jainism, Sikhism, Taoism and Hinduism. The concept of *ahimsa* — meaning non-violence, respecting life and doing no harm — plays a central role in Indian religions. *Ital*, the vegetarian and sometimes vegan diet of the Rastafari movement of Jamaica, is intended to improve health, avoid causing death and bring followers closer to what they refer to as universal energy and life force.

Gandhi wisely said that true happiness is when what you think, do and say are in harmony. When our diet and choices are in line with our belief system we feel our deepest values reflected in daily life. This is when we can live our innermost truth.

I know from experience that there is a soulful, authentic, joyful feeling when my outsides match my insides. And I'm not alone.

With 14 years' experience as a vegan, Grace from our A-Team explains what veganism means to her:

'Veganism is a philosophy on life. It reframes the way you see the world, see food and see yourself as a moral agent ... It's opened me up to world cuisine, made me think about the intersection of a variety of social issues like animal rights, human rights, migrant rights, environmental rights ... Veganism is a powerful idea ... one to which very few people can meaningfully provide any kind of robust counterargument, in my experience.'

Harry Bolman, host of *Vegan Hour*, a regular hour-long livestream on Facebook in which he interviews vegan identities, describes veganism this way:

'Veganism is the lifestyle that seeks to eliminate (as much as possible) the use of animals for any purpose ... To cease exploitation, enslavement, commodification and use of animals for any purpose. To treat all animals (and by extension, all living beings) with the love and respect we wish for ourselves. When our intention is to do no harm, we find a way, not an excuse.'

Why make this gargantuan effort to change our diet, clothes and beauty products in the first place?

Many of the world's greatest thinkers, like Pythagoras, Plato, Leonardo da Vinci, Rosa Parks, and Gandhi have been vegetarians or vegans.

People become vegan for a number of reasons, but there are three significant motivations to make the change:

- ❋ **Protect animals from cruelty.** Billions are trapped in lives of pain and suffering due to our exploitative industries. Small changes in our diet can directly save the lives of individual animals – creatures with a face, a personality, a mother, a child. Rather than exploit them for their bodily products, we can respect their rights to a life of freedom, dignity and value on their terms, not ours.
- ❋ **Stop the climate crisis.** Nobody wants it, least of all the polar bears stranded on icebergs, starving, as the glaciers melt around them. Raising animals for meat and dairy is one of the biggest contributors to global warming, surpassing even the transport and fuel industries for the amount of damage it causes.
- ❋ **Save the world.** Our Earth's last natural spaces and its precious wild species are in jeopardy. We are losing too many, too fast, and deforestation and pollution are primarily caused by animal agriculture. A vegan lifestyle is now regarded by scientists as a key tool for protecting the natural world.

Every month that we eat a vegan diet, we save about 125,000 litres of water, 543 kilograms of grain, 84 square metres of forested land, 273 kilograms of carbon dioxide and the lives of 30 animals.[1]

'If we could live happy, healthy lives without harming others, why wouldn't we?'[2]

Pam Ahern,
Edgar's Mission Farm Sanctuary

JEFFREY MASSON

Jeff is the author of numerous books, including *The Pig Who Sang to the Moon* and *Dogs Never Lie About Love*. He's also on the Voiceless Board of Directors and has been a vegan for 17 years.

MY GO-TO MEALS

Tofu and brown rice; Mexican burritos; Vietnamese rice wraps; a big salad with avocado. All quick and easy. Fresh, simple ingredients. Vegan, gluten-free, organic.

ON HONEY

Once in a while I have honey. Then I think about it and realise that bees want their honey and don't want to share it.

MY IDEAL WORLD IS

All vegan with no war and no corrupt leaders. Can we get there?

MY VEGAN INSPIRATIONS

Doing the research for my book on the emotions of farm animals, *The Pig Who Sang to the Moon*, inspired me. I saw how much chickens and cows suffered and I wanted no part of it. When I saw a cow crying out for her baby calf who'd been taken away from her to be slaughtered, it broke my heart.

THE MOST IMPORTANT THING TO REMEMBER...

How much suffering you're preventing and how good it is for your health and for the environment.

Protect animals from cruelty

What is your key motivation to start this journey? If you are concerned about animals, then you're in the majority. More people change their diet to protect animals than for the environment, their health or even the climate crisis. Melissa Hobbs, from The Vegan Company, says animal protection is number one for her: 'It's really about the animals – and the impact our choices have on our fellow sentient beings. I don't believe we need to eat or wear them, or use them in sport or entertainment. It's that simple.'

Seventy billion farmed animals are slaughtered around the world every year for human consumption, with most kept in conditions that cause them to suffer.[3]

Describing the immensity and intensity of pain that farming industries cause to animals is almost impossible to put into words. Acclaimed author Yuval Noah Harari puts it succinctly: 'The treatment of domesticated animals in industrial farms is perhaps the worst crime in history.'[4]

I've spent my entire life learning about cruelty to animals in farm industries and I still struggle to believe what they go through. The reason I changed my diet, clothes and lifestyle has always been and will always be to protect animals. This is true of many people I know, inspired by the famous 18th-century utilitarian philosopher Jeremy Bentham, who said, 'The question is not, Can they reason? nor, Can they talk? but, Can they suffer? Why should the law refuse its protection to any sensitive being?'[5]

While most people agree (including 95 per cent of Australians) that farmed animal welfare is a concern,[6] the parts of these industrial complexes that are considered the most ethically unacceptable are different for each person.

For me, what's most distressing is the psychological effects of permanent confinement on sensitive, social animals. It stops animals from having any kind of normal life – a 'battery' hen will never see the sunlight or be able to perform any of her natural behaviours such as make a nest, perch, roost, dig in the soil for worms, dust bathe, or lie in the sun.[7] I have rescue hens from battery cages who now live safely in my backyard and have witnessed how they derive great pleasure in doing all these things and more. Causing animals pain also upsets me deeply. Bodily mutilations without pain relief are standard practice in animal farming, with animals' sensitive tails, beaks and skin cut with knives and blades. Even castration occurs without pain relief. It's horrific.

Instead of respecting their lives, appreciating our differences and the wondrous diversity between species, animal-farming industries subject animals to a life sentence worse than the most violent criminals receive.

And it's not only urbanites cut off from the realities of farming who feel this way. Stories of farmers having their own 'aha' moments abound, despite the fact that farming animals at the same time as questioning your actions is an inherently difficult psychological leap. As Upton Sinclair wrote, 'It is difficult to get a man to understand something, when his salary depends on his not understanding it.'[8]

Nevertheless, the courageous tales include that of Sivalingam Vasanthakumar, a lifelong farmer in England, who was driving his 20 male lambs to the abattoir when he changed direction, heading over 300 kilometres to an animal sanctuary instead. Seeing the stress his lambs were suffering was finally too much for him to bear and he now farms vegetables. Bob Comis, an American farmer, switched to vegies after the connection he felt to his pigs made him question the morality of sending them to slaughter. A documentary of his journey, *The Last Pig*, chronicles this complex emotional journey.[9] Jay Wilde also took his animals to a sanctuary rather than a slaughterhouse – his epiphany forming the basis of the film *73 Cows*. Renee King-Sonnen loved ranching in Texas, but sending the calves to slaughter, and the wailing of their mothers calling for their babies for a week afterwards, made her question her actions. Today she runs an organisation that assists farmers transitioning out of animal farming and into other farming like veganic, wind or solar.

There are hundreds of similar stories, including those of farmers in New Zealand such as Jackie Scurr, who turned vegan after farming dairy cows, and Jennifer Barrett, a cattle and chicken farmer, who turned to farming mushrooms: 'I started to see the chickens differently. I'd never really looked at them as individuals before, but my heart started to break when I would see their terror and suffering. Suddenly I saw them as birds, not products.'[10]

These stories often come from family-run farms. However, the last couple of decades have seen a rapid decline in the number of farmers, an increase in the size of farms and a massive concentration of agricultural power in a few large corporations. For example, between 1970 and 2003 the number of Australian pig farmers fell by 94% while output grew by 130%.[11] Farms are now often vertically integrated systems where every stage of the process is controlled by the same few companies, and animals are merely a cog in a massive profit machine.

If you're reading this book, you are likely a person with great empathy who is interested in widening your circle of compassion, who sees the dissonance in our attitudes to dogs versus pigs when each can suffer equally. As I mentioned earlier, my epiphany came at age seven when I made the connection between my first pet dog, Bronnie, and other animals. Chay Neal, Executive Director of Animal Liberation Queensland, had the same experience: 'I went vegetarian around age ten once I decided that I would never hurt my best friend – a beautiful black Labrador cross – so why would I eat any other animal?'

Our experiences weren't unique. In fact, psychologists recently discovered that having a larger variety of pets as a child increases an individual's tendency to avoid eating meat as an adult. They found that growing up with pets makes us more concerned about how animals are treated. Renowned tennis star Martina Navratilova agrees: 'I did it for the animals. How can you have one animal as a pet and another for lunch?'

Of course, this isn't always the case. Many people consider themselves animal lovers (one American study found 74 per cent of people identify with this term), while believing 'food' animals are fundamentally different to pets. *Because animals are bred for our food, we can treat them worse* is a justification that enables us to kill billions of one kind while cuddling millions of the other. When we pick this belief system apart, the logic doesn't hold. It becomes clear it is cognitive dissonance, a mental block of our own making.

Just because an animal is bred for food, it doesn't remove their emotions or make them less likely to suffer pain – mentally or physically. We haven't bred out their inner lives, just changed their label from *pet* to *livestock*. Depending on which country you're from, a label may be entirely different. While people who follow a Judeo-Christian faith consider cows as livestock, in Hinduism they are sacred. Western countries now see whales as precious wildlife not to be consumed or used (only a recent phenomenon), while Japan calls out the hypocrisy as they consider kangaroos (which Australians eat) in the same category. Some cultures consume horses and dogs while others shun the eating of pigs. Our labels depend on us, our culture, religion and industries, not on the animals themselves.

But before we can feel empathy for animals, we have to understand them a little.

SENTIENCE

What is sentience? The word comes from the Latin verb *sentire*, which means 'to feel' and is related to *sensus*, meaning 'sense' or 'feeling'. For the longest time, we humans have imagined animals as stimulus–response machines and convinced ourselves that their inner lives are empty and barren. Today this is regarded by scientists as totally incorrect.

Animals have emotional lives, just like us, and they feel a similar spectrum of highs and lows. Individuals from a wide variety of species experience emotions ranging from joy and happiness to deep sadness and grief, along with empathy, jealousy and resentment.[12]

Researchers have discovered that many species of animals have the same neuroanatomical, neurochemical and neurophysiological substrates of conscious states as humans. They also have the capacity to exhibit intentional behaviours.[13] We are not unique in possessing the neurological substrates that generate consciousness; all mammals and birds and many other creatures, including octopuses, also have them.

Of course there are differences between humans and other animals. But the differences are not found in the emotional domain. This psychological wall we have built allows us to make laws and create mega-industries that differentiate us from animals, and farmed animals from pets. We categorise animals according to species, economic value and use, rather than their capacity to suffer. This wall allows a farmer to routinely cut off a pig's tail without any pain relief – something that would be against the law in many countries, including Australia, if done to a dog.

Over 90 per cent of Australians believe cattle, sheep, goats and pigs are sentient. It's hard to justify why we shouldn't treat pigs and dogs the same way when all the measures we would use to differentiate them – their intelligence, sensitivity, sociability and even domesticity – are equal.[14] The only distinction between a pig and a dog is whether they're inside or outside our circle of compassion.

Loving animals means loving *all* animals, not just the ones we share our homes with.

Fact: **Chickens experience REM when they're asleep, which indicates they dream.**

Adit Romano and Meital Ben Ari, founders of Freedom Farm Sanctuary, shared a story with me:

'Two little lambs, Maya and Jenny, came to our sanctuary refusing to drink from the bottle. We were very worried they wouldn't survive and managed to bring their mother, destined for slaughter a few days later, to the sanctuary too so she could breastfeed them. The mother arrived and was terrified of humans; she would hardly let us lead her into the sanctuary. But as soon as she heard the cries of her two babies, she rushed to their side positioning her body between us and them, protecting them from the harm she assumed we'd inflict. It was such a powerful moment that it made all of us cry. We realised more than ever that a mother is a mother and that maternal bond is the right of every creature. We have no right to take it away.'

If you need a reminder of why you want to become vegan, give your dog or cat a cuddle and remember that farmed animals are just as loving and sensitive as your pet is. Or go to an animal sanctuary and meet the creatures you're helping to save: with just one look (and a belly scratch) your decision will be confirmed.

ANIMAL WELFARE VERSUS ANIMAL RIGHTS

The divide between those who consume higher welfare animal products and those on a vegan path is symbolic of a difference in world view. There are hundreds of different ideas and philosophies on animals, but the biggest difference is between advocates of 'animal welfare' versus 'animal rights'. One looks at *how* we exploit animals, and the other looks at *whether* we should exploit them.

My father likes to ask poor unsuspecting people (often at a cocktail party), 'Is meat murder?'

Their reactions interest him. To put it simply, those who say 'Yes, meat is murder' arguably believe in animal rights, and the '*no*'s believe in animal welfare.

Animal welfare

An animal is in a good state of welfare if (as indicated by scientific evidence) it is healthy, comfortable, well nourished, safe, able to express its innate behaviour, and not suffering from unpleasant states such as pain, fear and distress. Good animal welfare requires disease prevention and veterinary treatment, appropriate shelter, management, nutrition, humane handling and humane slaughter. Animal welfare refers to the *state* of the animal; the treatment that an animal receives is covered by other terms such as animal care, animal husbandry and humane treatment.

For welfarists, it is morally acceptable for humans to use animals for our purposes, so long as they do not cause *unjustifiable* or *unreasonable* pain and suffering. So, for example, horseracing is okay, but using a painful whip may not be seen as necessary. The question of what is justifiable or reasonable suffering is, of course, highly subjective and depends on the animal's usefulness for humans.

Animal rights

Strictly speaking, animal rights refer to an animal's moral and legal entitlements. Animal rights advocates (sometimes referred to as 'abolitionists') argue that using animals for any human purposes, such as for the consumption of animal body parts and products (meat, fish, eggs, milk and so on) or for entertainment value (racing, performing, fighting and the like), is unacceptable.

To explain this better, take the analogy of murder, which is, in most cultures, considered wrong. If someone was charged with murder, the judge would care less about *how* they did it (was the murderer nice to the victim before the act? A Swedish massage, perhaps?) than *if* they did it (did the defendant take the life of someone who didn't want to die?). The sentence would be based on whether the defendant had intentionally killed the victim, not whether they made the murder as pleasant as possible. The same goes for animals: it's not how the farming or killing is conducted but the fact that animals are killed for our food, fashion or entertainment.

Although animal rights advocates don't all agree on the particular details, many believe that animals are entitled to enjoy fundamental rights, such as the rights to life, health and liberty. Accordingly, they challenge the property status of animals and disagree with the idea that it is morally acceptable for humans to use animals for our own purposes. In essence, animals have the right to live naturally without human interference.

Veganism fits neatly into this animal rights perspective by avoiding exploitation as much as possible. As Greg McFarlane, director of Vegan Australia, explains, 'Veganism is an ethical position with a corresponding way of living. The ethical position is that animals have the ability to suffer and that they have a right to their own body and life and not to be considered the property of others. The corresponding way of living is to avoid causing suffering to animals, as much as possible, and to actively strive to bring about a world where animals are not used by humans for food, clothing, entertainment or any other purpose.'

HUMANE AND FREE-RANGE FARMING

It's worth explaining a little more about the issues with the animal-welfare approach, how it differs from animal rights, and how I changed my perspective. With growing awareness of the horrors of factory farming, some farms are now promoting their 'humane' or 'free-range' products. These farms are celebrated in our communities by people who sincerely care about animal welfare because they aim to have less cruelty in their production methods, with improved housing systems, enrichment and varied access to the outdoors. These farms want to do better than standard industry practices — which usually fail to meet the basic international animal-welfare principles, coined 'the five freedoms'. The principles detail how farmed animals must be free from hunger and thirst, discomfort, pain, injury or disease; free to express normal behaviour; and free from fear and distress by farmers ensuring conditions and treatment that avoid mental suffering.

'Of course there is no such thing as "humane" animal farming. I've lived it; I know. Even on the smallest, most thoughtful of family farms like my grandparents' and great-grandparents' farms of "the good old days", the animals were and are used against their will and needlessly killed before their time. There may be opportunities to be "less cruel" but this does not amount to being humane.'[15]

Matt Bear, former farmer

When my father and I first started Voiceless back in 2004, we told our supporters that, although in an ideal world we should stop eating meat, dairy and eggs, if the change was too difficult, consuming high-welfare products was a good first step.

This is no longer our position. Although some farmers may have sincere, heartfelt intentions to provide animals with a better life and implement 'higher welfare' practices like allowing animals to move more freely and have access to the outdoors, many cruel practices are inherent to modern animal-use farming and can't be avoided despite the farmers' best attempts.

Here are some of the animal welfare issues that forced us to change our minds:

- ❀ **Male chicks.** Free-range egg farms may provide better living conditions for hens. However, they usually purchase their laying hens from hatcheries and breeder farms that, wanting only females, slaughter one-day-old male chicks as 'waste products'. Millions of these small, yellow, fluffy, adorable chicks are – rather than posted on Instagram as #toocute – gassed or macerated by high-speed grinders.
- ❀ **Pain.** In most countries, including Australia, there are no legal obligations for any farmers to use pain relief when engaging in husbandry practices which may cause pain. Practices such as tail docking, castrating, debeaking or teeth clipping, all of which cause immense suffering, are considered 'standard husbandry practices', so farmers can't be prosecuted for animal cruelty.
- ❀ **Transport.** Stress, fear and injuries, such as broken legs and wings, can occur during the land transport of animals from free-range farms to abattoirs.

Some countries, like Australia, have animal welfare standards and guidelines that govern live animal transport. However, animals like cows can still be transported for up to 48 hours and subjected to food and water deprivation, extreme temperatures and overcrowding before they are slaughtered.

✿ **Feedlots.** Cattle in Australia are often considered free-range, but this is misleading. Most of our supermarket beef comes from cows who spend their last months of life closely confined in feedlots to be 'fattened up'. Some feedlots provide shade, but because there is no legal requirement to do so, many don't bother and cows are left exposed to the elements. Cows are fed a diet of grain (if they've been in the feedlot for more than 100 days the meat is then called 'grain-fed') and a form of antibiotics to modify their rumen (the first compartment of a cow's stomach). Many feedlots plant hormonal growth promotants (HGPs) at the back of a cow's ear to make them gain weight very fast.

✿ **Lifespan.** Free-range animals are still killed early, normally in their babyhood or youth. A cow's natural lifespan is about 20 years, while those raised on dairy farms can be killed at 7 or 8 years old.[16]

✿ **Abattoirs.** Free-range animals regularly end up in the same slaughterhouses, or abattoirs, as factory-farmed animals, and the process of slaughter can cause great stress and fear. Countless undercover investigations have shown terrible cruelty in abattoirs in Australia and around the world, including beating, kicking, ineffective stunning and overuse of electric prods. Legislation for mandatory CCTV cameras in abattoirs has been passed or introduced in England, Scotland, Israel, France and parts of India, but despite lobbying, there are no CCTV cameras mandated in Australia.

We delegate the killing of animals to other people, placing the slaughterhouses way out of sight and mind. If we're not prepared to do it ourselves, or even bear witness, is it okay to give the task to others? *Game of Thrones* actor Peter Dinklage says, 'I wouldn't hurt a cat or a dog or a chicken or a cow. And I wouldn't ask someone else to hurt them for me.' Beatles star Paul McCartney famously said that if slaughterhouses had glass walls, everyone would be vegetarian. Susie Hearder from our Vegan A-Team agrees: 'At the age of 22, I went to an abattoir to see the killing process for myself and haven't eaten meat since.'

Even in the nicest of farms, the use of animals for commercial, for-profit purposes usually comes with a cost to the animal – suffering or pain. And, ultimately, even 'humane products' take an animal's life prematurely. Whether you consider that justified, necessary, moral or ethical is symbolic of a difference in world view and a question only you can answer.

I've talked a little bit about the difference between animal rights and animal welfare. Now I want to go into more detail about some of the animals most often exploited by humans.

The case for pigs

Pigs get the worst rap, with our everyday language full of negative associations, like accusing someone of being a 'dirty pig'. In fact, their nature is vastly different to what we are taught. Pigs are:

SUPER CLEAN

Pigs hate being dirty and keep their environment immaculate.

MATERNAL

Mother pigs build large nests to protect their young and they sing to their babies.

SOCIABLE

Just like us, pigs have friends they like to hang out with.

SMART

Pigs are cleverer than dogs and smarter than a three-year-old child (not that it actually matters, as all sentient animals, no matter how intelligent they are, deserve to be treated with respect).

Fact: **Pigs have 15,000 tastebuds while humans only have 9000.**

The exploitation of pigs is extreme. About one and a half billion pigs around the world are killed for meat every year, with most confined in factory farms.

FACTORY FARMING

Since their beginning in the 1940s, factory farms have become the most common system of producing meat, eggs and dairy at scale in many countries, like the USA, the UK and Australia. These intensive systems are also being adopted in rapidly developing countries including Brazil and China. While the word 'farm' conjures storybook images of open pastures and wicker, factory farming takes place under cover in massive complexes, often owned by big corporations. Tens of billions of animals, such as pigs, chickens, turkeys and ducks, are confined in conditions intended to maximise production and profits while minimising costs. These closed-door systems rely on the constant administration of antibiotics, artificial lighting, physical restraints and selective breeding. In the USA, factory farms are referred to as Concentrated Animal Feeding Operations (CAFOs).

Ten of the cruellest practices that we inflict on pigs are that we:

1. house them in closed barns devoid of sunlight or fresh air;
2. put pregnant pigs in cages so small they can't even turn around;
3. separate mothers from their babies with steel bars;
4. keep them on hard concrete floors, causing abrasions and sores;
5. use no pain relief to cut off their tails and shave their teeth;
6. never allow them to see the sky or even smell fresh air;
7. prevent them from ever feeling the earth under their trotters;
8. remove them from all normal social interaction;
9. prevent a mother from following her natural instinct to build a nest to protect her young; and
10. don't allow them to root in the earth (dig with their noses) like they love to do.

'I stopped eating meat some 50 years ago when I looked at the pork chop on my plate and thought: this represents fear, pain, death.'[17]

Dame Jane Goodall DBE

My father, Brian Sherman, visited an enormous factory farm for pigs just before we launched Voiceless. It was, like the vast majority of pig farms in Australia, foreign-owned by a large corporation, rather than family-run. This would be one of the few times we were allowed entry into such a place – once industries got wind of our active concern for animals, the 'veil of secrecy' was promptly lowered and any access denied.

Even Australian journalists find locked doors as they attempt to research farming practices. Chef and author Matthew Evans writes, 'This is an industry that is afraid of scrutiny. Afraid of transparency.' He goes on to say, 'Those who rear and breed and control the most intensive farms across the land think we have no right to know what is done in our name. I wonder, do they think they are above public scrutiny?'[18]

I didn't join my father on this trip as I was pregnant with my daughter, Jasmine, and it was believed that the high concentrations of toxins in the air could be dangerous for her wellbeing. My worries weren't unfounded.

For schoolteacher Bente Jørgensen, who lives next door to a pig farm in Denmark, the 'smell is so awful that it makes me feel sick. My head aches and my eyes are red and swollen. I feel that our lives are destroyed because of the smell, noise and dust from the farm.'[19]

This is my dad's account of his day at the farm – hardly a scene out of *Charlotte's Web* or 'Old MacDonald Had a Farm':

A tiny piglet clambers towards me, slipping and sliding over the backs of his mates in his crammed enclosure. By the looks of him, he must be just a few weeks of age, new to this life. He has the *joie de vivre* of the very young. Arriving at the barrier that separates us, he turns up his face towards me, lifts himself on his haunches and places his front feet on a rail, snuffling my hand and reaching down to sniff my feet and legs through the steel bars. His snout twitches at my unfamiliar smell and his small body vibrates with excitement: he has a read on this interloper.

The inquisitive little fellow is ready to talk. 'What's up, mate?' he asks me with his eyes. I crouch and scratch him under the chin. He squeezes his eyes shut, stretches his neck and cocks his head to one side in delight. But the news is not good.

'I'm sorry, mate. There's nothing up.'

I don't have the heart to tell him the full truth. He has no life. The fact is that the four windowless walls of his shed

will remain the outer limits of his universe. He will spend his allotted time on its harsh metal floor, not a scrap of straw or clod of earth in sight, artificial lights buzzing overhead, the cacophony of the thousands of others confined here filling the putrid air.

His mother, separated from him, will lie broken and half-mad in her prison, a tiny concrete-floored, steel-barred sow stall no larger than her body, until she exhausts her capacity to produce one litter after another and is killed. In a few months, they will cram her baby onto a road train and truck him out, perhaps a long distance, perhaps over days. He will travel in freezing rain, or in blazing heat without a drink to quench his thirst. When he arrives at his destination, they will manhandle him into a slaughterhouse chute, where he will listen to the screams of his dying mates as he cowers in confusion and terror or fights with all his might before he is prodded towards his violent and premature death.

He will never do the things that make him a pig: feel the grass or solid ground underfoot, roll in the cooling mud, snuggle with his mother and siblings in the straw, root and forage in the earth, or use his five senses to take in the big world. No sun will warm his back as he runs. His first glimpse of daylight will be through the slatted bars of the slaughterhouse truck. Everything that will happen to him will defy nature and fly in the face of decency.

'I'm so sorry, mate. That's it. *Fin.*'

I look over to his slightly older counterparts in an adjoining pen. Their time is running out. Some chew furiously and repetitively at a bolt hanging from a crossbar on their cage. It's the only game in town; there is nothing else for them to do. Others stand or lie inert on the floor, or mill aimlessly about in the crush of the enclosure. I turn back to the little pig. Ours is an uncomplicated connection, wordless and fleeting, but I feel it profoundly. The species barrier is a fiction here, an imaginary fence the food-animal industry erects to secure humans' dominion and to absolve us of our crimes. We are simply two sentient beings.

This chap is clearly endowed with a keen intelligence. He has a lust for life and a complex emotional repertoire that is his alone. In this, he is like us, like the dogs and cats we love as family, and like all other pigs, whose capacity for thought and feeling is comparable to that of a three-year-old child. He feels happiness, fear, hunger, thirst, pain and longing, as we do. And he is utterly and completely defenceless, totally at our mercy. In all probability, mine is the first and only kind touch he will receive.

I wear the foreknowledge of his miserable fate, of the injustice of it, heavily, like a cloak of grief. It is all I can do to stop myself from shouting to the heavens: It is ungodly! It is unbearable! This is not life!

And we have no right to impose it on any living creature![20]

DR MIRYAM SIVAN

Miryam is a writer, teacher and academic who was vegetarian for 40 years before going vegan.

ADVICE FOR NEWBIES

We're creatures of habit and this includes our diet. A person who's used to pouring cow milk in their morning coffee can also get used to having a milk alternative. Once you adjust to eating a new way, it's not a big deal; it soon becomes your norm and then there's no stress or 'issue' surrounding it. It's the same thing the entire day.

The other piece of advice I'd give is to not press the point with friends and family. Lead by example and not necessarily by strident advocacy. I think there's a place in our world for activism, but in one's personal circle – especially if this is the beginning of the vegan life – I think it might be better to use that energy to strengthen the position inside and not get into discussions and (inevitable?) conflict with others on the outside.

MY JOURNEY

I always loved animals and was deeply attached to the dogs we had. At 13, I made the decision that I didn't want to eat animals, but this didn't go over well in my house. So, I postponed this life decision until age 17, when I moved out. When I was in high school, I spent time with sheep and lambs, and I'm convinced that no one who eats lamb chops ever held a lamb in their arms. About 7 years ago, a beloved yoga teacher told me that since I was 80 per cent there anyway, I should consider going vegan. But I felt attached to my occasional cheese and egg dish. One day I came home and my teenage daughter was weeping in front of the computer, watching videos of the animal industry. I went in to comfort her, watched a few minutes of a video and was absolutely horrified. I remembered Isaac Bashevis Singer's famous comment that for the animals, every day was Treblinka. We both became vegan at that moment.

BEST COOKING TIP

Fresh produce! I love to roast vegetables and it's so easy. Just cut them up, sprinkle with olive oil and salt, and stick them in the oven. I read somewhere that to eat well there should always be a cooked grain and a cooked vegetable dish in the fridge. I live by that. I alternate vegetable dishes and rotate these grains: rice, buckwheat, barley, bulgur and freekeh (made from green wheat – delicious!).

MY FAVOURITE MEALS

Green salad (always ... at every meal!) along with lentil soup. Hummus and majadra (lentil–rice dish) and roasted vegies ... whatever is on hand. Recently, I made a fabulous lasagne with cashew cheese. Wow. Has to be on the favourite list.

MY IDEAL WORLD IS ...

Vegan. And I'm not the only one who thinks so. In Genesis, Adam and Eve were given plants and not animals to eat. It was only after the Flood, according to the text and its many commentators, that people began to eat meat (and live shorter lives). In an ideal world, we would also not use animals' skins for our clothing. There are plenty of plant-based, and other, materials that can function well, even for shoes. In an ideal world, people would be held more accountable for the way they treat domesticated animals, including pets. In an ideal world, we would understand that we're not above the animals, just like we're not above plants and trees. Our ignorance of how other beings experience life is vast. I hope the more we know about them (like now with trees and their root networks), the easier it will be for people to feel compassion and empathy, and to grasp how all of life on our planet – and possibly beyond – is interconnected on a moral, spiritual, and yes, even cellular level.

THE HIGHS AND LOWS OF VEGAN LIFE

The high is knowing I'm not contributing to cruelty in such a direct way. Of course I, and everyone around me, contribute to cruelty in our world by purchasing cheap goods, etc. made at the expense of other people's work conditions and lives. I try to consume less and to buy fair trade. There are no lows. There's the discomfort sometimes of being a guest in other people's homes and knowing they're flustered by veganism in a way that they're not with vegetarianism. So in these cases, I tell hosts to just cook vegetarian. Oftentimes the food ends up being vegan anyway, and if not, I may or may not eat some because I think it's also important not to offend my host. This only holds true with cheese ... I'd never eat flesh of any kind to spare a host's feelings.

CHICKENS - FROM NEST TO NUGGET

Until recently, like most people, I knew little to nothing about chickens. In fact, being the urbanite I am, I hadn't ever really met one. I didn't realise that chickens are playful, curious and enjoy dust baths, sunbaking and scratching in the soil looking for tasty treats. I didn't know they keep one eye out for predators while the other searches for food, and I didn't understand that a pecking order is serious business, or that they invite their friends to share food with a high-pitched staccato call.

Fact: Chickens demonstrate syntax and semantics, once considered exclusive to human language.[21]

Despite dedicating my life to advocating for animals, I had never truly communed with a feathered creature. Until I met Feather, my first rescue hen. She was thrown out of a battery farm because of a leg injury, rescued by a local passer-by, taken to a temporary foster home and eventually found me.

I quickly learned how to scratch under Feather's large feathers to discover tiny ones beneath and feel the roughness of her comb. It surprised me that she liked to sleep in trees (I'd often find her snoozing in the top branches of a neighbouring pine): after all, she'd never seen a tree or flown before, having been locked up her entire life in a battery cage. She had a special vocalisation that she used every time she'd see me coming, and we bonded.

I still have hens roaming in my garden, and one of my favourite things in the world is hanging out and watching them live their best lives. They lay eggs – depending on the season and their mood – which my family shares with them (they love eating their own eggs and need the extra calcium). When friends visit, I'm ready to answer the inevitable questions: Don't you need a rooster to make eggs? How do you know which egg will be just an egg or which one a chick? Are chickens smart?

'The mechanized environment, mutilations, starvation procedures, and methodologies of mass-murdering birds, euphemistically referred to as "food production", raise many profound and unsettling questions about our society and our species.'

Karen Davis, PhD[22]

Here is what I now know about chickens: Chickens, as we think of them today, are our own human creation. The most common species, *Gallus gallus domesticus*, was domesticated from four species of wild jungle fowl: colourful birds that once roamed the tropical forests of South-east Asia. About 10,000 years ago, people began to keep these creatures captive, using them for everything from egg-laying to bird-fighting.

Chickens like to sleep in tree branches, perch on bushes, forage for insects, make nests, bathe in dust, play and, like most of us, hang out with their friends. Chickens are sentient animals and can experience pain and suffering as well as fear, anxiety and even boredom. Although they have a reputation for being 'brainless', increasingly they're being discovered to be amazing creatures. Chickens communicate using over 24 different types of vocalisations, and mother hens show an emotional response when witnessing their chicks experiencing pain or making mistakes.

One study concluded that they have the attributes of empathy. There's evidence that chickens possess the capacity for long-term memory and eavesdrop on each other. They can tell their own social standing in the flock by observing how other birds interact and comparing themselves to others.[23]

Today chickens are the fastest growing choice for meat in the world and among the most exploited animals on our planet. Chickens are ranked first place by scientists for the saddest of all prizes – they have the *worst* life experience of all animals used by humans, both wild and captive. Sixty-five billion chickens are eaten every year worldwide, with most raised in intensive farming, living in crowded windowless sheds and fed a regular diet of antibiotics. In addition to distress, chickens in commercial industries suffer from diseases and injuries, which cause pain, as well as overcrowding and poor environmental quality.[24]

Broiler (or 'meat') chickens

They may not be housed in cages, but tens of billions of chickens slaughtered for meat are crowded into closed sheds, unable to perform even their most fundamental natural behaviours like moving freely, roosting and nesting. The chicken sheds are full of ammonia. Wet litter is used on the floor and the chemicals it contains can cause hock burns, ulcerated feet and breast blisters. Feed restrictions are imposed on the broilers used for breeding, which lead to chronic hunger. 'Meat' chickens have been selectively bred to grow at a very fast rate and are slaughtered at 35 days old rather than living for seven to ten years as their relatives do in natural environments.

Battery hens

Battery hens spend their entire lives in cages in artificially lit sheds that hold tens of thousands of birds. These conditions are designed to maximise laying activity and increase profit. Cages are stacked on top of each other, and each hen has between three and 20 cage mates and a space smaller than an A4 piece of paper. She can't perform natural behaviours like wing-flapping, grooming, preening, stretching, foraging and dust-bathing.

Battery hens may experience chronic pain from the development of lesions and foot problems caused by standing on the sloping wire floors designed for egg collection. Extreme inactivity results in hens developing disuse osteoporosis, leading to chronic pain from bone fractures.[25]

Due to the suppression of many of their natural instincts and social interactions, such as choosing a suitable nesting place to lay their eggs, battery hens can become frustrated, fearful and aggressive, which triggers behaviours such as henpecking, bullying and cannibalism.[26] In an attempt to prevent this behaviour from causing injuries to other hens, producers routinely conduct beak-trimming or 'debeaking' on chicks using no pain relief. This most commonly involves the amputation or searing off of a portion of the sensitive upper and lower beak using an electrically heated blade. Re-trimming may also be carried out if a hen's beak grows back.

Debeaking causes tissue damage and nerve injury, particularly in older birds. In addition to the pain caused by amputation, scientists believe the process can cause the beak to develop long-lasting and painful neuromas, or tumours.[27]

One of the most awful, and least known, aspects of egg production for all production systems (including free-range) is the mass slaughter of male chicks. As males can't lay eggs and have not been selectively bred for their size or meat quality, they are generally considered unsuitable for meat production and are slaughtered following hatching.

The permitted methods of slaughter include carbon dioxide gassing or maceration (the grinding of live chicks). In Australia as many as 12 million male chicks are killed this way each year.

Where do eggs come from?

I'm regularly asked, 'But why don't you buy free-range eggs?' I gently explain the killing of male chicks and other welfare issues with commercial industries, and often the vegan-curious continue to ask me chicken-related questions, particularly about eggs. Many people have never met a chicken and find it perplexing as to how eggs come about in the first place. Here's a breakdown of which comes first, the chicken or the egg. Let's first cover eggs and how they're made.

Inside a hen's ovary, as with human gals, there are many ova (eggs). And, also like us, a hen is born with all the eggs she needs for her lifetime. On a regular natural cycle (but only if she has 14 hours of light, which means chickens won't lay during short winter days), one ovum is released from its follicle (known to us as the yolk) and travels into the oviduct. Have you noticed that there's a tiny white spot on an egg yolk? That's a single female cell called a blastodisc. Now, this is where a rooster (also known as a cockerel or cock) can become important. If the hen hooks up with a rooster and makes love, sweet love, this spot is fertilised and an embryo begins to form. If there's no rooster in sight, albumen (egg white) forms around the yolk. Now in the uterus, the egg gains its shell, a process that takes about 20 hours. The hen then looks for a quiet, safe nesting area to lay her egg. If a rooster has mated with the hen, the egg is fertilised. In a natural setting, the hen will sit on her egg, keeping it warm, turning it and even talking to it with purrs and clucks (chicks know their mother's voice!). Three weeks later, a chick is born. Hens stop laying eggs as they get older, mimicking our female menopausal experience.

Now let's look at where the laying hens (used in commercial farms, from battery to free-range) come from. First, hens and roosters are put together in large sheds to mate. The hens then lay their eggs, which are now fertilised. The eggs are collected and, rather than the hen sitting on her egg and nurturing her chick, they are put into machines in hatcheries, which are buildings with controlled ventilation. The egg (containing the growing and still unborn chick) is moved through different machines until it hatches. The small chicks are then transferred from the machine to the examination and 'sexing' system, which can be on an automatic conveyer belt. This is the point where males are taken away and killed through maceration or gas while the females have their beaks cut and are packed into trucks to be sold to the egg industry. These are some of the reasons why I believe that any commercial egg production is ethically questionable.

FISHES

About three trillion fishes are caught in the wild or farmed each year.[28] To understand how our industries affect them, we first need to get to know our underwater friends.

For the grammar nerds (love you guys!), I'm using the word 'fishes' and not 'fish' for a reason. There are at least 33,230 different species (from sharks to manta rays), and many scientists believe referring to such a huge number of disparate fish as one singular entity, rather than a plural, is weird. Clumping them together also encourages us to see them as a commodity rather than the individuals that they are.

In recent years, scientific evidence has increasingly shown fishes as intelligent, socially sophisticated and capable of experiencing pain and suffering.[29]

'Me and my siblings witnessed fish being killed in a really violent and aggressive way and it was just really obvious that that was something we didn't want to participate in and we didn't want to support ... I don't want to cause pain to another living empathetic creature.'

Joaquin Phoenix, vegan since the age of three[30]

Senses

Fishes' senses (taste, smell, sight and hearing) are highly tuned. They have a refined taste, holding the record for the highest number of taste buds (not only in their mouths but on their bodies too). A shark can smell 10,000 times better than us humans, and a salmon can smell the equivalent of a single drop of water in an Olympic pool. Fishes can see and differentiate colours more vividly than humans. Some have such developed hearing they can eavesdrop on the ultrasonic sounds made by dolphins (who may be hunting nearby), and discriminate between music genres. Fishes can make a variety of sounds (including hums, whistles, grunts, croaks, purrs, clicks, chirps, growls and snaps)

by vibrating their swim bladders, grating their teeth, rubbing their bones together, expelling bubbles and more. Female cod and haddock even choose males based on their drumming ability (a muscle that vibrates on their swim bladder), while minnows may shout at each other during aggressive exchanges.

Social lives

Fishes are the most sociable of animal groups and lead complex social lives. They often live in a social hierarchy, recognise individuals and are careful when choosing mates. When protecting their territory, fishes are aggressive to strangers but tolerate familiar neighbours. They cooperate when shoaling or schooling, have complex relations within species and families, and show many examples of inter-species cooperation. There are many anecdotes of fishes displaying compassion for other fishes who are disabled or in distress. For example, fishes have been seen to gently guide and aid tank mates who are having a hard time with swimming or buoyancy.

Tools

For a long time, we thought only humans could use tools. We were very wrong. The list of tool-using species has expanded over the years to include many other mammals, birds and fishes. Scientists have discovered that fishes don't only use tools; they actually build homes with rocks or coral, or by using bubbles or mucus. There's a type of minnow that selects and gathers 300 identical pebbles to act as bricks and a wrasse that can build a new rocky house every night. Some fishes build elaborate and decorative structures, patterns and mandalas to impress potential mates. Who needs hands when fishes have fins and mouths to move and arrange sand or other objects? Tuskfish can use a rock to crack open clams, and other species use rocks to crush sea urchins or carry their eggs. One species lays its eggs inside a mussel so the bubs are protected until they are ready for the open ocean. A whopping 9000 fish species build nests!

Pain and suffering

We have been led to believe that fishes are 'unconscious' and 'unfeeling' because they lack a neocortex. But this has been disputed by scientists who believe fishes have all the hardware needed to have the same experiences as us animals with a neocortex.[31] A group of scientists signed a Declaration on Consciousness, concluding consciousness isn't only limited to vertebrates. Rather, emotions can derive from parts of the brain other than the cortex, and affective states can still be felt without a neocortex.[32] Fishes have all the biological and physiological systems necessary for pain perception and they show all of the behavioural markers of feeling pain. They learn to detect and avoid painful stimuli and when in pain they become distracted from simple tasks or everyday behaviour. Fishes also respond positively to pain relief, and studies show they are willing to pay a cost to get it (certain fishes chose an otherwise less desirable tank because it provided a painkiller).

Commercial fishing

Ninety-seven per cent of all animals slaughtered for food globally are fishes. Over the past hundred years, an estimated 80 per cent of the biomass of fishes (the number of fish multiplied by their weight) in the world's oceans has been lost. Experts predict the numbers of wild fishes will be completely depleted by 2050.

This is because we're not talking about relaxing on a boat with a fishing rod here. The fishing industry is high-tech and uses sonar, satellite navigation, depth sensors and maps of the ocean floor to maximise the yield. Bycatch also presents a serious issue as non-target species such as turtles, seabirds, dolphins, whales and seals are caught indiscriminately by purse seines (huge nets), longline fishing and bottom trawling, and are often thrown back into the ocean, injured or dead. Also, 74 per cent of ocean entanglements of sharks and rays are caused by so-called ghost fishing gear – dropped or discarded equipment.

Fishing isn't only a welfare concern; it affects the health of our oceans too. Today, how many fishes we take from the ocean is no longer limited by how many it's possible to catch, but by how many there are left to be taken.

FIVE FISHY SKILLS

If you haven't already guessed, fishes are amazing! Here are more things they can do.

Navigate like champs. Some fishes use the angle of the sun or tune into the Earth's magnetic field to navigate their way through the water.

Communicate quickly. Fishes have keen electroreception abilities, the fastest form of communication in the animal kingdom. A shark may be able to sense the heartbeat of a fish hiding 15 centimetres under the sand.

Learn well. Fishes perform almost any feat of learning that mammals and birds can do and have even outperformed primates in solving certain puzzles.[33]

Recognise themselves. The classic test for self-awareness is the 'mirror self-recognition test', and, if an animal passes, the species is celebrated as having complex cognitive abilities. In the past, only humans, elephants, dolphins, crows and ravens could do this. But in 2018 a species of fish passed the mirror self-recognition test. Welcome to the club, cleaner wrasse fish!

Remember things. Fishes can recognise and remember individual humans even after several months, something which many humans would find tricky!

Fish farming

Aquaculture is the fastest growing animal-use industry in the world, with between 51 to 167 billion fishes farmed each year. By 2021 aquaculture is predicted to produce more than half the fishes consumed around the world.

Like factory farming of land animals, there are many serious welfare issues associated with aquaculture. These include intensive confinement, artificial conditions, overcrowding and an inability to perform basic natural behaviours, with fishes suffering systemic injuries, deformities, diarrhea and stunted brain development. Wild-caught fishes are the main food source for farmed fishes, with 87 per cent of the global production of fish oil used in aquaculture. Fish farms also contribute to the spread of viral and bacterial diseases and parasites such as sea lice, which cause massive die-offs of wild fishes. On Canada's coast, sea lice infected 80 per cent of wild pink salmon, impacting salmon-dependent wildlife like bears, eagles and orcas.

Fact: **Archerfishes aim and spit sharp jets of water through the air to catch insects up to 3 metres away. This requires a great deal of skill because of the visual distortion that occurs when looking from water to air, so archerfishes have to learn distortion patterns to determine target size and position.**

HONEY BEES

I didn't know much about honey bees until I started researching this book. Learning about them has been fascinating.

Honey-bee hives are unbelievably complex, with tens of thousands of bees working in a harmonious symphony in highly specific, sophisticated and complementary roles. Scientists still don't know enough about them, other than they have a unique and complex form of communication that involves sight, motion and scent. They're capable of abstract thinking,[34] can recognise family members, map their travels and memorise new pathways and sources of food.

The question of honey and its impact on the welfare of bees is one that many people, including myself, have found a teensy bit confusing. Now that I understand what the issues are with their individual and group welfare, let me break it down for you.

Honey bees are a species of bee that have found their tiny yellow selves subject to massive industry use. This is because they're particularly productive in a way that we commercially minded humans tend to appreciate. Unlike wild bees, which are often way better pollinators, honey bees produce honey in a manner we can easily harvest on a mass scale.

Because we know so little about the inner lives of bees, it's hard to assess the impact of our honey industry by observing emotions in them such as fear, stress or pain, and we can't use the same scientific indicators we would normally employ to measure the welfare of animals like cows or pigs. However, there are several obvious reasons why commercial honey production would compromise these beautiful buzzers, and colony collapse disorder, which scientists link to bee management stress, is a clear indicator that there are serious issues.

Bees make their prized nutrition-packed syrup as back-up food for the winter, when they need extra sustenance; a little like trusty squirrels stashing away their nuts in the forest. When we take bees' supply of winter food and replace it with sugar water, a substance with few of the same qualities, this leaves our bee friends in a vulnerable position, susceptible to disease.

Just like in farm-animal industries where old animals have less economic value and are slaughtered early, the queen honey bee is often killed long before her seven-year life span is up and replaced by a younger bee. As with other industries where animals are mutilated without pain relief for the sake of easy profit, the queen can have her wings clipped to prevent her swarming or starting a new colony (a natural behaviour that allows bees to reproduce but reduces honey production). Bad handling of bees can, similar to hens, cause torn wings and legs, and queen bees, like dairy cows, are often artificially inseminated.

Along with killing, injuring and clipping bees, we also manipulate their environments, forcing them to nest close to the ground rather than up high, and changing the geometry of their colonies. We do this because not having to climb trees to access the honey is convenient for mass production. Without further study of bee sentience, it's difficult to know the psychological stress this change of elevation may cause, however we do know that this stress can trigger disease.

Some vegans let honey slip off their priority list, but given the clear and present danger to bees, there's no good reason to continue eating honey when there are so many delicious alternatives. Now I know what bees go through, I mostly stick with agave syrup as my bee-friendly sweetner. Rice syrup and maple syrup are other alternatives.

SOMEWHERE

This is an extract from the inaugural speech of the honourable Emma Hurst, MLP, NSW Parliament.[35]

Somewhere a mother cow is crying for her newborn baby. She will cry out for him all night until her voice goes hoarse, and she can no longer bellow. She will be impregnated again soon so she continues to produce milk. Her little boy was sent to slaughter as he is useless in the dairy industry. Last year on a BBC documentary a dairy farmer broke down in tears and admitted that some mother cows cry for days when their calves are taken.

Somewhere a pig bites at the metal bars of her cage. She recently gave birth on the cold metal flooring. She cannot interact with her young because her cage won't allow such movement. She is more intelligent than the dogs we have in our homes. If given the chance she could learn how to play soccer, or video games,

and show us that she is capable of love and friendship. Instead, she repetitively rocks against the cage bars that are creating welts on her skin. She has gone mad.

Somewhere a chicken has just fallen.

Her legs too weak to hold her obese body any longer. They now splay out in front of her. She sits in the build-up of six weeks of faeces from tens of thousands of other chickens. The faeces will soon start to burn through her feathers and then her skin. She would stand to avoid the pain, but she is no longer able. She has been bred this way and she'll be in chronic pain for the last days of her life.

DAIRY - IT'S NOT WHAT WE IMAGINE

We have been raised to believe, thanks to billions of dollars spent by dairy industries on marketing, that drinking cow's milk is not only good for us but also actually good for cows, that we're doing *them* a favour. If they're not milked then they'll be in pain. That's what I always thought; what about you? When I first questioned and understood the absurdity of this belief, my mind was blown.[36]

Let's take it back to basics. In a natural setting, female cows mate with male cows, get knocked up, have their babies (aww, cute) and begin their journeys as mothers. Mother cows, like women after childbirth, produce milk with the biological imperative of feeding their babies. This milk is the perfect mixture of nutrients that their bub needs to grow and eventually it dries up when their calf becomes independent and able to feed itself.

In order for us humans to acquire a mother cow's milk in commercial quantities, we have to do two things. First, we need to remove her baby so we can access the milk instead of the calf doing so. And second, we need to keep the female cow in a state of perpetual impregnation and birth so that her milk never dries up. Both of these activities, most notably taking her babies away, causes a mother cow great stress and grief. A mother cow can bellow day and night in search of her calf, often returning to the place where the calf was last seen.

Another deeply unpleasant fact about the dairy industry

is that it causes the death of millions of baby male calves, also known as 'bobby' calves. In Australia, approximately 800,000 male calves are killed each year. These calves can't be used to create milk (for obvious reasons) and because of their breed they're not great for meat either. So they're transported off to abattoirs as babies and killed at about five days old. They are purely waste products in the eyes of the industry.[37]

Former New Zealand dairy farmer Katie explains what bobby calves are:

'A calf who has no monetary value to the dairy industry due to being the wrong sex, the wrong breed, or simply surplus to the needed numbers of animals. These innocent babies, who don't ask to be born, are picked up by a truck at four days old and taken to their deaths. Bobby calves are animals who are quite literally born to die. The babies aren't 'needed', but their mothers are required to give birth to them so that they will produce milk for the farmer. Their babies are then killed at the earliest convenience ... The mother cow, naturally horrified and distressed out of her mind, chases alongside the trailer, bellowing and calling to her baby, while the confused and terrified calf cries back to the mother.' [38]

DR SY (SIAW-YEAN) WOON

Sy is an Australian veterinarian who graduated from the University of Sydney and is now based in the USA.

MY JOURNEY

I've been vegan for eight years (almost one-third of my life!). I was inspired by my love for animals and my realisation that it was hypocritical to claim that I loved all animals while continuing to support the exploitation and consumption of certain species. Moreover, as a veterinarian, it doesn't make sense to devote my life's work towards saving certain animals' lives and yet paying for other animals to be killed so that I can have them on my plate.

HOW I BEGAN

I've loved animals ever since I can remember and always wanted to avoid hurting them. When I discovered that veganism existed, this lovely ideal, I wanted to pursue it. But everyone told me I'd be malnourished. The food industry and media told me veganism wasn't feasible. In Australia 10 years ago, there were far fewer vegan options and education available compared to now, where we're spoiled for choice.

Being a vet student and exposed to the routine practices of the animal agricultural industry also gave me first-hand insight into the inherent cruelty of this corporate sector. Examples include painful beak trimming, castration of baby lambs and cows without analgesia and chopping off piglets' tails – once again, without any pain relief. We'd learn about these standard practices as if they were a necessity and these 'farm' animals were presented to us (by our professors) as if they were devoid of the same emotional capacity that dogs and cats possess. Such lessons served to justify these inhumane procedures and desensitise us vet students.

At the same time, pre-vegan, I was president of the University of Sydney Animal Welfare Society and liaising with various animal rights organisations presenting

these same standard practices for what they are: unnecessary, inhumane and largely hidden from the public eye.

During my required dairy placement, I witnessed the forced separation of newborn calves from their loving mothers, all for the purpose of taking the mother's milk for humans to consume. The sadness expressed by both mother and baby was palpable.

At 20 years of age, I made the connection at last and became vegan. Finally, I felt that my values and my love and respect for animals aligned with my actions and my leadership position. Learning that various alternatives to non-vegan food existed and that I didn't have to merely survive on garden salads was also helpful in my transition to veganism.

TOP MEALS

BBQ jackfruit tacos, any kind of Indian-style curry, and creamy pesto pasta. Notable mentions include garlicky vegie pizzas, thick green smoothies, and sushi.

MAKING FOOD

When starting out, I recommend avoiding complex recipes that have 20 or so ingredients; there are so many easy vegan recipes you can try that take less than an hour – most Mac and Cheese recipes, smoothies, red sauce pasta dishes and pizzas with pre-made crusts (most crusts are automatically vegan!).

— Fight climate change —

A plant-based diet is recognised as *the* key tool that everyday people, like you and I, can use to combat climate change. This is because the negative impacts of animal agriculture on our climate are now well known.

The Intergovernmental Panel on Climate Change (IPCC) states that human-made effects are extremely likely to be the leading cause of global warming since the mid-20th century, and that 'continued emission of greenhouse gases will cause further warming and long-lasting changes in all components of the climate system, increasing the likelihood of severe, pervasive and irreversible impacts for people and ecosystems'.[39]

'Shifting from animal meat to plant-based meat ... is one of the most powerful measures someone can take to reduce their impact on our climate.'[41]

Leonardo DiCaprio, actor and environmentalist

The animal agriculture sector emits 18 per cent, or nearly one-fifth, of human-induced greenhouse gas emissions. This is more than the entire world's transportation sector, including the combined exhaust fumes from every vehicle on Earth.[40] And not only that, animal agriculture and its use of land creates more greenhouse gas emissions than the generation of power.

For those of us passionate about stopping climate change, we can reduce greenhouse gas emissions by a whopping 35 per cent by eliminating meat from our diet. Changing our diets could stop global temperatures from rising the predicted two degrees Celsius above pre-industrial levels.[42] It is the most powerful decision we can make. People who eat a diet high in meat cause 7.2 kilograms of carbon dioxide emissions per day, compared with 3.8 kilograms caused by vegetarians and just 2.9 kilograms for vegans.[43]

The impact of farming animals for food on climate change first became a concern in 2006 with the publication of a damning report by the United Nations (UN) called *Livestock's Long Shadow: Environmental Issues and Options*, which identified animal agriculture as having a substantial contribution to 'climate change and air pollution, to land, soil and water degradation and to the reduction of biodiversity.'[44] But it took many years for this shocking information to be absorbed into the public arena.

Before founding Voiceless with Dad, I worked for one of the world's largest environmental NGOs (non-governmental organisations) that valiantly battle the biggest environmental threats. However, even though the UN report had already been published, the impact of meat and dairy was never mentioned or addressed by the NGO's leaders or in any written materials. I was one of the few vegetarians on their plentiful staff.

Fortunately, things have moved on and today the contribution to climate change of greenhouse gases from farm animal industries is acknowledged and widely discussed.

Many people who once considered themselves meat-eating environmentalists are altering their diets, and the world's largest NGOs are, albeit slowly, integrating messages of the environmental benefits of plant-based diets into their agendas. Jonathan Safran Foer aptly puts it like this – 'We cannot keep eating the kinds of meals we have known and also keep the planet we have known. We must either let some eating habits go or let the planet go. It is that straightforward, and that fraught.'[145]

Save the world

Veganism can save the world – I'm not even kidding. That's a big statement, but it's true.

According to leading scientists, going vegan is the single biggest way to reduce our personal impact on the Earth. Paul McCartney agrees: 'If anyone wants to save the planet, all they have to do is just stop eating meat.'[46]

Eighty per cent of our planet's total farmland is used to rear livestock. This vast amount of land used for meat and dairy production poses multiple problems. The following are some of the most significant ones.

RAINFOREST DESTRUCTION

Livestock and feed crops are the leading driver of rainforest destruction with 55 million hectares (136 million acres) of rainforest worldwide cleared for animal agriculture.

Remember the Amazon burning in 2019? It wasn't an exceptional fire; in fact, large tracts of the Amazon are burned each year. The Amazon has 40 per cent of our Earth's tropical forests and 10–15 per cent of its biodiversity.[47]

Fact: One in ten known species in the world lives in the Amazon rainforest, making it the largest collection of plants and animals on Earth.

CNN's headline about the fires went viral: 'The Amazon is burning because the world eats so much meat'.[48] The news stunned the world – cattle ranchers and loggers were responsible for most of the fires, clearing the pristine rainforest so they could raise cattle for meat or grow soy to feed their livestock. This has been on public record since the 1980s (aptly coined 'the hamburger connection'). Cattle ranching is the largest driver of deforestation in every Amazon country, accounting for 80 per cent of current deforestation rates. Amazon Brazil is home to approximately 200 million head of cattle, and is the largest beef exporter in the world, supplying about one quarter of the global market.

Soy cultivation is also a major driver of deforestation, but not for our soy lattes or tofu. Seeds from the soybean plant provide high-protein animal feed for livestock, and 80 per cent of Amazon soy is destined for animal feed.[49]

OVERUSE OF LAND

Meat and dairy animals now account for about 20 per cent of all terrestrial animal biomass, and around 30 per cent of the Earth's land surface is currently used for livestock farming.[50] Since food, water and land are scarce in many parts of the world, this is a totally inefficient use of our precious resources. Almost half the world's crops are fed to livestock, but only 15 per cent of the plant calories end up being eaten by humans as meat. If everyone chose to go vegan, global farmland use could be reduced by 75 per cent, freeing up land mass the size of Australia, China, the European Union and the United States combined.

SPECIES EXTINCTION

Humanity has wiped out 60 per cent of mammals, birds, fish and reptiles since 1970. We are in the midst of the Earth's sixth mass extinction.[51] The organisation that wins longest name of the year, the Intergovernmental

Science-Policy Platform on Biodiversity and Ecosystem Services (IPBES) found that around one million animal and plant species are now threatened with extinction, which could occur within decades. And there are more threatened species today than there have ever been before in human history.[52]

The average abundance of native species in most major land-based habitats has fallen by at least 20 per cent, mostly since 1900. The picture is less clear for insect species, but evidence suggests that an estimated 10 per cent are threatened. More than 40 per cent of amphibian species, almost 33 per cent of reef-forming corals and more than a third of all marine mammals are threatened. At least 680 vertebrate species have been driven to extinction since the 16th century.

> 'You can't be an environmentalist, you can't be an ocean steward, if you're not eating a plant-based diet.'[53]
>
> James Cameron, film maker and environmentalist

Why is this devastating rate of extinction happening? The loss of wild areas to agriculture is the leading cause of the current mass extinction of wildlife, and animal agriculture contributes significantly to deforestation. Livestock graze on huge amounts of land and also consume enormous quantities of feed crops (grown specifically for them). Both of these activities contribute to biodiversity loss.

The many benefits that a healthy ecosystem provides us – known as 'ecosystem services' – are things like clean water, regulating our climate, forming soil, pollination of plants, and nutrient cycles like oxygen. Sounds pretty important, right? Well, thanks to livestock, 60 per cent of our Earth's ecosystem services are in decline.

Australia is no exception. Land clearing for livestock puts Australia on the top of the list of deforestation hotspots. In one year in Queensland alone, 45 million animals and 400 million trees were killed. At the rate of current clearing, the next 15 years will see an area just under the size of Tasmania razed. The environmental organisation WWF (World Wild Fund for Nature), expects koalas to be extinct by 2050. A move towards a vegan diet significantly lessens the amount of wild land lost to agriculture, which is one of the leading causes of mass wildlife species extinction.

LAND DEGRADATION

Livestock cause wide-scale land degradation around the world, with about 20 per cent of pastures considered as degraded through overgrazing, compaction and erosion. This figure is even higher in the drylands, where livestock contribute to advancing desertification. Desertification is a process where fertile land turns into desert due to drought, deforestation or inappropriate agriculture. One-third of the world is becoming desertified, with livestock as *the* leading factor.

WASTING WATER

Animal agriculture uses vast quantities of water for the production of animal feed. We need to feed a cow about 15,000 litres of water and 25 kilograms of grain to produce 1 kilogram of beef.[54] Widespread overgrazing also disturbs water cycles, above and below ground, reducing replenishment of water resources. Here's a statistic to connect this data with our lives: we save more water by skipping one serve of chicken for dinner than forgoing six months of showers.

POLLUTION

Factory farms discharge immense amounts of pollution; it seeps into our groundwater system and pollutes the air with toxic waste particles and ammonia, causing a flow-on effect of problems. Manure run-off from factory farms in the United States has polluted 56,300 kilometres of river in 22 states. The livestock industry pollutes our global fresh-water sources and marine ecosystems and destroys our coral reefs. This causes eutrophication, with too many nutrients moving from the land to water, and the death of animal life from lack of oxygen. The major polluting agents are animal wastes, phosphorous, nitrogen, antibiotics and hormones, chemicals from tanneries, fertilisers and the pesticides used to spray animal feed crops.[55]

Top scientists agree that avoiding meat and dairy products is the best way to reduce your impact on the planet. Our environment cannot sustain the amount of meat and dairy we are currently consuming, with its associated destruction and pollution of land, water and air. And consider this: our population is predicted to reach 10 billion by 2050.

Let's return to the question *why go vegan?* The answer is (sadly) simple: the future of our Earth and all its creatures is in our not-so-humble human hands. Do we want to create a world devoid of all other life forms and natural habitats? A world where we fight for the last drops of clean water, struggle to grow crops in degraded dry soils? Swim in oceans emptied of life? Do we want a world where climate change has led to further sea-level rises, elevated temperatures, droughts, hurricanes, human devastation and even more species extinction? In this less-than-pleasant future picture, the only animals we will witness (assuming humans survive) will be taxidermied in a museum or enclosed in a zoo or aquarium, and people will struggle to recall memories of natural forests, coral reefs and flowing rivers. As David Attenborough says, 'What we do in the next few years will profoundly affect the next few thousand years.'[56]

Let's stay hopeful. You can, I can, we all can make a difference and change our ways, change our future. And we can begin today.

3

HEALTH
& FOOD

'I am living without fats, without meat,
without fish, but am feeling quite well
this way. It always seems to me that
man was not born to be a carnivore.'

ALBERT EINSTEIN

*This chapter was written in collaboration with
Dr Leila Masson, medical doctor and paediatrician.*

Today millions of people around the globe are proving that being healthy and being vegan are highly compatible. A healthy vegan diet is appropriate for all stages of our life, including pregnancy, breastfeeding and adolescence. Research shows that vegetarians and vegans are at reduced risk of a number of health conditions including heart disease, certain cancers, Type 2 diabetes, hypertension and obesity.[1] This is because vego and vegan diets are often low in saturated fat and high in vegetables, fruits, whole grains, legumes, soy products, nuts and seeds (all of which are rich in fibre and phytochemicals). This causes both lower total and low-density lipoprotein cholesterol levels and better serum glucose control, which leads to the reduction of chronic disease.

A large, comprehensive study of nutrition, informally known as the 'Grand Prix of epidemiology', concluded that human beings are basically a 'vegetarian species' and, for our own health and longevity, we should stay clear of meat and dairy.[2]

Expert scientific advice regarding diet usually recommends fewer animal products but, unfortunately, some nutritionists haven't caught up with the times. Others rely on information from health studies surreptitiously funded by meat, egg and dairy industries who use questionable science or draw suspect conclusions.[3] A number of people I know have also increased, rather than decreased, their meat consumption following trends such as paleo and low-carb diets. And many ill-informed health professionals scare away their vegan-curious clients, making them doubt their decision to adopt a vegan diet. Make sure you're getting advice from only the most informed and educated experts.

— Disease and longevity —

Going vegan can help your health flourish: studies show veganism can be beneficial for the following health problems:

- ✿ **Cancer.** Research links the consumption of meat, especially red and processed meats, to increased risk of several types of cancer, while evidence suggests that vegan and vegetarian diets are a useful strategy for reducing the risk of cancer.[4] The science is so compelling that comedian Jon Stewart and film director James Cameron joined a push to add breast cancer warning labels to cow's cheese.[5] The campaign, Let's Beat Breast Cancer, was created by the Physicians Committee for Responsible Medicine, a US non-profit organisation advocating for a plant-based diet as preventative medicine. The 12,000 supporting doctors are urging the United States' public health regulator, the Food and Drug Administration, to make consumers aware of the dangers of consuming cheese, which contains concentrated amounts of estrogen, the primary female hormone.

- ✿ **Heart disease.** Scientists have discovered that people following a plant-based diet have a 40 per cent reduction in their risk of death from both cardiovascular disease and coronary heart disease and their hypertension risk drops by 34 per cent.[6] Heart disease is the leading cause of death worldwide, and a large American study published in the *Journal of the American Heart Association* found that people who ate the most plant-based foods had a 16 per cent lower risk of suffering a heart attack, stroke, heart failure or other heart-disease related condition.

❄ **Obesity.** Clinical trials and observational research show evidence of the advantages of plant-based diets for preventing obesity and promoting weight loss.[7]

A vegan lifestyle could also increase your chance of living a long life. *National Geographic* reported that the world's three longest lived tribes were vegetarian. Hamida Musulmani, at one stage the world's oldest person, worked on her farm until the ripe age of 126, having lived a vegetarian diet for a long time. According to the Guinness World Records, the oldest person in 2006 was China's 120-year-old Du Pinhua – a lifelong vegetarian. Vegetarians often feature in 'oldest people alive' lists.[8]

Fact: Donald Watson, who came up with the term 'veganism' in 1944 and started the first vegan society, lived on a plant-based diet until the ripe old age of 95 and took great pleasure in outliving all his critics.[9]

SARAH MARGO

Sarah is an animal lawyer who's passionate about social justice for all beings and the environment. She's been vegan for eight years.

MY CHANGE TO A VEGAN LIFE

I was raised vegetarian for compassionate reasons. For a long time, I mistakenly thought that eggs and dairy were non-harming by-products. When I learnt about the reality of the egg and dairy industries, I realised that being vegetarian for compassionate reasons didn't fully make sense, so I went vegan. I think most people believe in the vegan philosophy but don't realise how their actions are contradictory. I'm much happier now and consciously adapt my diet and lifestyle as I continue to learn about how my personal choices impact beings and the environment.

HOW I CONNECTED WITH VEGANS IN THE EARLY DAYS

I joined a local community group for vegans which frequently held events. I then went to a lot of vegan restaurants, markets, festivals and activism events – there's always a community of animal lovers nearby!

THREE THINGS NEW VEGANS SHOULD KNOW

One: you can replicate any meal in a cruelty-free way. Two: your food repertoire actually widens, and you open up to a whole new world of cooking and flavours. And three: it's easy!

ON HEALTH

Vegan junk food isn't any healthier than non-vegan junk food!

IF YOU'RE FEELING OVERWHELMED

Institutionalised animal suffering can be hugely distressing. It's so important to seek out support if you feel overwhelmed. Remember, too, that you're not alone – there are millions of people who think like you and are doing amazing work to better the world.

Social conditioning

Most of us have been raised on messages that animal products are essential to our diet, especially in Australia where we are the second highest meat-eaters in the world.[10] But this assumption is not correct – science is now catching up and proving the case for a plant-based diet.

Director of Vegan Australia, Greg McFarlane, talks about his experience:[11]

> 'I had been brainwashed by years of tradition, advertising and animal agricultural lobbying to believe that my body needed meat and other animal products. I then discovered that this was far from the truth and that I had been lied to all my life.'

Melissa Hobbs from The Vegan Company says, 'There are heaps of myths, perpetuated by powerful industry bodies who want to keep you eating meat and dairy.'[12] According to clinical psychologist and academic Kelly Brownell, past strategies used by tobacco industries have been adopted by food industries, or 'Big Food', today. These tactics include dismissing peer-reviewed studies that report public health issues and paying scientists for pro-industry research. They also target children with advertising and conduct intensive political lobbying to stop regulation.[13]

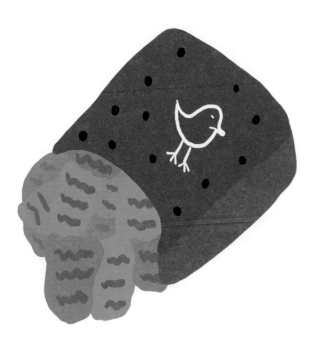

— Strength and fitness —

It was well known in ancient Greece that Olympic athletes performed best when they ate plant-based diets. And today, top athletes from all sporting disciplines are going bananas for a vegan diet. In terms of strength, endurance and fitness, you can't argue with the world's best boxers, weightlifters, marathon and sprint runners, tennis players and surfers – athletes from every discipline. Scott Jurek, world-renowned record-breaking ultramarathon runner, says, 'My accomplishments were achieved not in spite of, but as a direct result of putting animal products in the rear view. No beef, no chicken, no pork, no fish, no milk, no cheese, no eggs. Just plants.'

'I've found that a person does not need protein from meat to be a successful athlete. In fact, my best year of track competition was the first year I ate a vegan diet.'

Carl Lewis, Olympic sprinter, Olympic athlete of the century

Other superstar athletes agree that being vegan gives them the best performance. These include tennis legend Martina Navratilova, footballer Jermain Defoe, five-time Formula One world champion Lewis Hamilton, and bodybuilder and Mr Universe Barny du Plessis. Australian cricketer Peter Siddle and his wife, Anna Weatherlake, are both outspoken vegans. Morgan Mitchell, an Australian 400-metre and 800-metre runner selected for the 2020 Tokyo Olympics, says as soon as she went vegan she even started beating the boys on the track. Then there's the outstanding example of Fauja Singh, who set the world marathon record for age 100 and over in 2011 as a vegetarian.

David Haye, a British boxer with world titles in two weight categories, says, 'It's a myth that you need meat for strength.' American snowboarder and three-time Olympic medallist Hannah Teter believes her plant-based diet has opened up more doors to being an athlete: 'It's a whole other level that I'm elevating to. I stopped eating animals about a year ago, and it's a new life. I feel like a new person, a new athlete.'[14] Tia Blanco, two-time winner of the Open Women's World Surfing Championship, adopted a vegan diet because of her love for the environment, the sea and animals, which was brought about by her passion for surfing. Tia says: 'I feel really great eating a plant-based diet and love the way it makes me feel physically and mentally. Many of us know the effects of diet on one's health, but fail to realize that diet plays a huge role in more than just your personal well-being.'[15] As four-time NBA champ John Salley says, all the 'smart' athletes are going vegan.[16]

Reading about vegan athletes certainly inspires me to be the best vegan I can be. How about you?

CHAY NEAL

A long-time vegan, Chay is Executive Director at Animal Liberation Queensland.

MY JOURNEY

I first went vegetarian at age nine after realising I would never hurt my dog, Beau, a black Labrador that we adopted from the RSPCA. Beau was a remarkable animal to spend much of my childhood with, with such love, trust and loyalty. If I wouldn't eat my dog, why would I eat a pig?

Nine years later, I looked more into the egg and dairy industries and made the connection. I realised that I had to be vegan if I wasn't to contribute to harming and killing animals. While living at home, I started cutting back on dairy and eggs and the next year, when I was 19, I moved out of home and that day I went completely vegan. It was definitely one of the best decisions I've ever made.

'Vegan' was a much lesser known term back then. I was disappointed that there were no animal rights groups at university, but soon got in touch with local organisations and individuals and became an activist. I learned that as a vegetarian you will save some lives (or rather, spare some lives); as a vegan you will save even more; but as an activist, you have the chance to really influence others and thereby save millions.

It was through veganism that I also met my amazing wife, Felicity. After many years of friendship we married at a beautiful vegan wedding in 2014. And in 2015 we had a beautiful daughter, who's being raised vegan – healthy and full of energy!

Being vegan has never been easier. Today there are countless social media groups as well as face-to-face social groups. In most cities, there are animal rights and vegetarian/vegan groups that you can get involved in or seek support from. Most coffee shops offer soy milk and most restaurants have at least some dishes that can be easily made vegan. There are new vegan and vegan-friendly restaurants and cafes popping up all the time. There are physical and online shops where you can buy a vegan version of just about anything you had as a non-vegan. And there are programs like the Vegan Easy Challenge or Challenge 22 to offer you tips and recipe ideas as well as provide access to mentors to make your vegan journey even easier.

DON'T GET OVERWHELMED

Remember why you're vegan. It isn't a purity contest or a vegan 'club'. Cut out meat, dairy and eggs and then start to consider some of the by-products. I've seen many people get overly focused on minor by-products (out of good intentions) but this can sometimes be counterproductive. It can end up becoming overwhelming. I believe it's important to keep the animals at the centre of veganism, rather than a list of ingredients. Personally, I try to be as vegan as possible – I'll research the wine I buy, check ingredients at supermarkets, but I also want to make veganism as accessible as possible. When dining with friends, I would certainly ask to ensure there's no meat, dairy or egg in any of the cooking, and perhaps enquire a bit further, but I certainly wouldn't refuse to eat until I've inspected every label.

Eating well

Going vegan, despite the effort, is a joyful and positive culinary experience. Yes, changing your tastes and eating habits can be hard, especially letting go of a few beloved dishes, but it is extremely rewarding. Here I want to give you a few key tips that will make sure your change to veganism is nourishing, healthy and easy.

Begin your journey in the healthiest way possible by adding nutritious delicious foods rather than narrowing your diet or increasing processed junk. Abundance is the ticket. After all, there are reportedly over 70,000 edible plants to choose from! This is an opportunity for dietary expansion (rather than scarcity) and you will be surprised and delighted by the new tastes, textures, exotic ingredients and even sweets that will make you swoon. The best way to do this is to add new daily foods into your diet, veganise your favourite meals, and stock up your kitchen with staple ingredients and delicious go-to snacks.

But what do you have left to eat? is a common refrain from friends and family. Animal lawyer and longtime vegan Sarah Margo responds with an internal eye-roll and the thought, 'A wider variety of food than you!' My dear friend, vegan foodie Issie Saker, says sweetly in response, 'I never lack anything tasty to eat.'

In a nutshell, any issues that may arise from swapping to a vegan diet often come from restricting and reducing your variety and this is best avoided by making sure you add a food each time you remove one. So, if you take beef out of your diet, add beans. Remove fish, add tofu.

Shaun Moss from our Vegan A-Team says, 'Let "greens and beans" be your motto and you'll be lean and healthy.' He describes his vegan food journey:

'The most important thing I didn't know was where to get calories, and at first when I got really hungry I would binge on high-carb foods like bread and pasta. I needed to learn to include plenty of legumes, nuts and seeds in my diet, and to avoid refined carbs as much as possible. The next step after vegan is 'whole foods vegan', which I believe is a very important and oft-ignored step in dietary improvement in terms of health.'

Choose vegies and legumes and skip the white bread, white pasta, sugar and chips, which give you calories but no healthy micronutrients. How can we add more vegies to our diet? Try adding them to a salad, soup, wrap, curry, smoothie, pasta sauce, rice, or vegie burger, or dip them in a spread such as hummus.

Gemma Davis, Voiceless Ambassador and vegan naturopath, says, 'Eat a wholefood-based diet. More from the Earth, less from packages.' Another Vegan A-Team members adds: 'It's not enough to stop eating animal-based products and only eat pasta and potatoes – you have to make sure that your new diet contains all the important nutritional values.'

Seeing a dietician or health practitioner who is knowledgeable about plant-based diets may help provide ideas and guidance. It's also worth seeing a doctor to get some baseline tests done so you can see any health changes as your vegan journey progresses.

Author and publisher Kathy Divine suggests new vegans take a reference blood test for iron, B12, folate, calcium and more:

> 'Not because the vegan diet is lacking, but to illustrate to yourself and others that a well-planned vegan diet can adequately meet dietary needs. Take the test at the time you decide to go vegan and then do a follow-up after a few months to see any changes. Tweak your diet if needed. Consult a well-informed health professional if you need to increase your intake in a certain nutrient. This health professional may not be your primary doctor. Consult someone with experience with, and who is in support of, vegan diets.'[17]

Following vegan food bloggers, recipe sites, YouTubers and nutritionists online has helped me and so many aspiring vegans begin positive habits. But I also agree with the opinion of one of our A-Team, Grace Prael, who says:

'Do not use social media or anecdotes as definitive sources of nutrition information. Always seek out scientific consensus where available. If you find scientific information too technical, consult high-quality sources that translate scientific findings into information useable by the general population ... You can also try googling a topic and including 'study' or 'research' in your search terms, then carefully selecting sources that way.'

So, do your research, focus on nutrient-dense whole foods, and try to add in one food for every one you remove (remember, abundance!). And, yes, a vegan cupcake is beyond delicious and a plant-based burger essential to my wellbeing, but all in moderation. I discovered that eating healthy is eating healthy, junk food is junk food, and processed is processed, even if it's vegan. The same rules apply.

Miriam Cumming from the Vegan A-Team suggests not buying junk food because that way 'you won't have it in the house when you're at your weakest'. Rather, she says, 'cook simple meals from scratch so you know there isn't hidden salt, oil or sugar.' Kathy Divine agrees: 'Avoid the temptation of the growing number of vegan junk-food products on the market. They are so deliciously delicious, but reserve them for special occasions like birthdays and holidays.' Kathy also recommends avoiding faddish YouTubers and instead consulting people who have studied nutrition at a university-degree level or equivalent.

Although you could always live by Oscar Wilde's philosophy: 'Everything in moderation, including moderation.' Sometimes we all have to go a little wild!

VEGAN NUTRITION

Nutrition is an important part of eating well. The most common question vegans are asked is, 'Where do you get your protein?' Major concerns also include iron and calcium. Don't worry, I've got you covered. Let's break down all the components you need to feel confident you have your nutritional bases secured.

Most of us are creatures of habit, looking for routine in all areas of our lives, including what we eat. Creating your weekly vegan meal plan so it's balanced isn't too hard if you find a handful of dishes that you like and can regularly make. We do need to be aware that the daily food pyramid for vegans looks a little different.

Here's one example of how it can look:[18]

- ✿ 5+ servings of carbs and starchy vegies
- ✿ 4+ servings of vegies
- ✿ 3+ servings of beans and lentils
- ✿ 2+ servings of fruits
- ✿ 1–2 servings of seeds and nuts
- ✿ and a B12 supplement.

Colour

Eat rainbows and you'll find the pot of golden health!
No, really – different coloured plant-foods have different
phytochemical compounds and these compounds have
major benefits for your health. Here's a rainbow of
delicious food (I'm sure you can add more to the list too!):

- ✿ **Red:** tomato, strawberry, apple, watermelon, raspberry, cherry
- ✿ **Orange:** carrot, orange, sweet potato, apricot, squash
- ✿ **Purple:** eggplant, beetroot, plum, grapes
- ✿ **Yellow:** lentils, bananas, lemons, peaches
- ✿ **Green:** broccoli, edamame, spinach, peas, avocado
- ✿ **White:** potato, tahini, oats, chickpeas, lima beans, soybeans, tofu, onion, quinoa
- ✿ **Brown:** cashews, lentils, almonds, hazelnuts, pistachios, peanut butter, mushrooms, dates
- ✿ **Blue:** blueberries
- ✿ **Black:** black beans, chia seeds.

Proteins

The Recommended Dietary Allowance of protein is
0.8 grams per kilogram of body weight per day.
So if you're 65 kilograms, for example, that's
65 times 0.8, which equals 52 grams of protein
per day. You can use one of the many
online protein calculators to find out
what the number is for *your* body.
But don't get too stuck on data –
research on how much protein
is the optimal amount to eat for
good health is ongoing, and the
debate is far from conclusive.[19]
There is no need to consciously
combine different plant proteins at
each meal because as long as we eat
a variety of foods every day, our body maintains a
pool of amino acids that can be used to complement
dietary protein.[20]

Check out the list below of healthy proteins and include
them in your everyday eating, but please don't sweat
it. Contrary to popular belief, this is not an issue. A
comprehensive medical review found vegans with
protein deficiency were *far from the norm*.[21] Here are
some great protein-rich foods to add to your diet:

* **Seitan:** 25 grams of protein per 100 grams. It's
  made from gluten, the main protein in wheat. Unlike
  many soy-based mock meats, seitan resembles

the look and texture of meat when cooked. I use it regularly, adding garlic, fresh tomatoes and herbs, to make vegan bolognese.

🌸 **Tofu, tempeh and edamame:** 10–19 grams of protein per 100 grams. All originate from soybeans. Soybeans are considered a whole source of protein, providing the body with essential amino acids. Tofu is made from soybeans ground in water and then heated. The curds are pressed into a block, which can come in various forms from silken to firm. (Soft tofu can be added to miso soup while firm is delicious cooked in oil or roasted in the oven.) Tempeh requires the cooking and fermenting of soybeans before they are pressed into a patty. Tofu easily soaks in the flavour of the ingredients you use to prepare it (such as miso sauce or coconut milk), while tempeh, often found ready-prepared in the supermarket, has a nutty flavour. Edamame are immature soybeans that need to be steamed or boiled before you eat them. You can buy them frozen or order them with a sprinkle of salt in your favourite Japanese restaurant.

🌸 **Lentils:** 18 grams of protein per cup, cooked. While lentils provide about 2.1 million calories per acre of land used, chicken meat, the most 'efficient' animal product, only provides 1.4 million calories per acre.[22]

🌸 **Other pulses and pseudograins:** examples include chickpeas – 15 grams of protein per cup, cooked; lima beans – 15 grams per cup, cooked; and quinoa – 11 grams per cup, cooked.

🌸 **Green peas:** 8 grams of protein per cooked cup.

These are an awesome addition to your diet and they're also super high in fibre and vitamin K and good for your eyes.

❀ **Vegetables:** the most protein packed include broccoli, spinach, asparagus, artichokes, potatoes, sweet potatoes and brussels sprouts with about 4–5 grams of protein per cooked cup.

❀ **Nuts:** a handful of mixed nuts is my favourite protein-rich (and calcium-rich) snack. Almonds have 6.4 grams of protein per 28 grams (about a handful) while for the same portion size, peanuts yield 7 grams, pistachios 5.5 grams, pecans 2.7 grams, sunflower seeds 6.4 grams and flaxseeds 5 grams.

❀ **Nutritional yeast:** 8 grams of protein per ¼ cup. Many of our A-Team noted it as an essential pantry item in the kitchen because of its cheesy flavour and because it's a complete protein containing many B vitamins and trace minerals.

Fact: **Seitan is made by washing wheat flower with water and has been used as a meat substitute in China since the sixth century.**

Calcium

We need calcium for our bones, and it doesn't need to come from dairy. Apart from the issues with animal cruelty and environmental destruction, dairy is associated with lots of health problems ranging from bloating, diarrhea and allergies to iron deficiency. Dairy is also linked to higher risks of some cancers, like prostate.[23]

Vegans can have a higher risk of bone fractures, so please be sure to eat calcium-rich foods. Luckily there are lots of healthy calcium sources: tahini, calcium-fortified non-dairy milk drinks, such as soy, rice, coconut, oat or nut milks. Read the label to see how much calcium you get in a serving. Your daily calcium requirement depends on your age – teens need up to 1300 milligrams while adults under 50 require 1000 milligrams. Over 50 and your body needs 1200 milligrams.[24] Here are some top calcium sources:

- ✿ **Soy milk, enriched:** 250–450 mg per cup.
- ✿ **Cooked soybeans:** 261 mg per cup.
- ✿ **Soybeans/edamame:** 98 mg per cup, cooked.
- ✿ **Raw firm tofu:** 683 mg per 100 grams.
- ✿ **Broccoli:** 62 mg per cup, cooked.
- ✿ **Beans:** 370 mg per cup black-eyed peas; 191 mg per cup white beans.
- ✿ **Tahini:** 130 mg per 2 tablespoons; also high in magnesium, potassium and iron.
- ✿ **Almonds:** 97 mg per ¼ cup, and brazil nuts, 35 mg per ¼ cup.

- ✿ **Almond butter:** 111 mg per 2 tablespoons.
- ✿ **Kale:** 177 mg per cup, cooked.
- ✿ **Cereals**, **calcium-fortified:** ranges 250–1000 mg per ½ to 1 cup.
- ✿ **Chia seeds:** 160 mg per 2 tablespoons.
- ✿ **Flax seeds:** 36 mg per 2 tablespoons.
- ✿ **Orange juice, fortified:** 300 mg per 348 mg per cup.
- ✿ **Figs:** 300 mg per cup, dried or uncooked.
- ✿ **Butternut squash:** 84 mg per cup, boiled.
- ✿ **Raisins:** 54 mg per ²/₃ cup.

Iron

In good news, the American Dietetic Association confirms vegetarians don't have a higher incidence of iron deficiency than non-vegetarians.[25] And one of the most comprehensive studies ever undertaken into the relationship between diet and the risk of developing disease found that the consumption of meat is not needed to prevent iron-deficiency anaemia.[26]

However, it's always a good idea to have your iron levels checked. If it's low, stock up on more iron-rich food or take a supplement. Green leafy vegetables (ideally three servings per day) are a good start, and adding something with a little vitamin C (orange juice, broccoli or tomato) will help to increase the absorption of iron. The recommended intake varies, but for menstruating women it's 14–18 milligrams per day. For men and non-menstruating women it's about 8 milligrams. Here are some good sources:

- 🌸 **Tofu:** 6.6 mg per ½ cup,
- 🌸 **Quinoa:** 2.2 mg per 150 grams, cooked,
- 🌸 **Spinach:** 6.4 mg per cup, cooked,
- 🌸 **Kidney beans, chickpeas, soybeans, lima beans:** 4.5–5.2 mg per cup, cooked,
- 🌸 **Black beans, pinto beans:** 3.6 mg per cup, cooked,
- 🌸 **Pumpkin seeds:** 3 mg per 30 grams,
- 🌸 **Peas:** 2.5 mg per cup, cooked,
- 🌸 **Potato with skin:** 2 mg per 1 medium,
- 🌸 **Brown, red, green lentils:** 6.59 mg per cup, cooked,
- 🌸 **White or cannellini beans:** 5.2 mg per cup, cooked,
- 🌸 **Dark chocolate:** 7 mg per 85 grams.

Vitamins and minerals

Vitamin B12 is the only must-have supplement for vegans. It is crucial for the maintenance of our nervous systems and formation of red blood cells.

B12 is made by bacteria (or anaerobic microorganisms) living in soil and water, rather than animals or plants. Animals consume the bacteria by eating grass with soil particles attached to it. The bacteria then accumulate in their gastrointestinal tract until absorbed into the muscles of their bodies. While in the past, humans would have ingested B12 in the same way animals do – by eating plants like roots and tubers that had traces of soil – today that's not the case. Our current agricultural systems incorporate cleaning and sanitisation, plus our soil is exposed to antibiotics and pesticides – all practices that rid our food plants of bacteria. Back in the old days, we would also have drunk from streams and wells which would have contained B12-producing organisms. In modern society, the chlorination of our water has removed B12 (as well as many other disease-causing bacteria). It's because these natural B12 sources no longer exist that vegans must consume B12 as a supplement. You can buy B12 in drops or tablets.

You may want to consider other vitamins and minerals with advice from a natural health provider (I take a daily multivitamin just to cover my bases as I don't like to measure or count grams and milligrams). For example, zinc can sometimes be low in vegans so it's important to get your levels checked. Omega 3 is important for good mood, brain power, learning and concentration, and linseeds, flaxseed and canola oil, chia and walnuts are all great sources. But some people are not efficient at converting those into the highly beneficial long-chain omega-3 fatty acids, DHA and EPA, and need to take them as supplements. Traditionally found in fish, you can get your Omega 3 just as easily from a non-toxic (organic) algae oil.

NUTRITIOUS AND DELICIOUS FOOD

Preparation will make your vegan journey much smoother – if you have everything you need in the pantry and a good list of go-to snacks and simple, tasty meals, you'll be surprised at how easy the process will be. Don't worry, the trusty Vegan A-Team and I will share all our best ideas and practical tips so you'll be sure to have delicious vegan food at all times!

Kitchen must-haves

I try to include essential ingredients in my diet as a matter of daily habit. Here's a list of my must-haves and those of our A-Team members.

My friend Issie makes the most delicious vegan food ever and her must-haves include quinoa, a good olive oil, tomatoes, broccoli and seasonal fresh vegies. She believes in one essential item for the freezer: 'With a frozen packet of mixed vegies you'll always be able to make a meal. Fry them with olive oil and garlic and you can add it to quinoa or rice, or make a quick, easy pasta sauce.'

When you try new foods, don't judge on first taste; it takes repeated experiences for your taste buds to adapt and to know if you like something or not. Don't give up!

Pantry

- ✿ **Nuts:** almonds, cashews, pistachios, walnuts, hazelnuts and more. Make a jar of mixed nuts and enjoy a handful as an afternoon snack.
- ✿ **Oats:** a good winter breakfast. Add nuts, seasonal fruit and agave syrup for sweetness.
- ✿ **Split peas:** a delicious base for a hearty soup.
- ✿ **Chia seeds:** can easily be transformed into a delicious breakfast pudding with fresh fruit.
- ✿ **Seeds:** flax, hemp, sunflower, pumpkin. Add to salads and smoothies.
- ✿ **Quinoa:** a great basis for a salad with cucumber, onion, seeds and dried cranberries.
- ✿ **Canned or dried legumes:** chickpeas, lentils and more. Add black and kidney beans to a dollop of rice and roll into a burrito. Enjoy it with guacamole on the side.
- ✿ **Lentils:** delicious in a soup or tortilla wrap.
- ✿ **Tahini:** mix raw tahini with water, garlic, lemon and salt to be drizzle on food.
- ✿ **Nutritional yeast:** sprinkle over pasta, use as a cheese substitute in sauces, or add as a thickener for soups and sauces.
- ✿ **Coconut milk:** use in soups, curries, smoothies and even muffins.
- ✿ **Spices and sauces:** soy sauce, tamari, hot sauce, rice vinegar, mustard, apple cider vinegar, sweet chilli and more.
- ✿ **Lentil flour:** good for flatbread, muffins and omelettes.
- ✿ **Vegetable stock:** a pantry must-have.

- ✿ **Oils:** olive oil, sesame oil, grape seed oil and other healthy oils.
- ✿ **Dried fruits:** for snacks and cakes.
- ✿ **Pastes:** laksa, tom yum, red curry, miso and so on.
- ✿ **Sheets of seaweed:** add to rice bowls, soups, salads and burgers.
- ✿ **Dark chocolate:** just yum! And good for cookies and mousse.
- ✿ **Dried mushrooms:** for sauces and stews.
- ✿ **Wakame flakes:** good in miso soup or mixed into rice.
- ✿ **Vegan mayonnaise:** dollop on a burger.
- ✿ **Syrups (to replace honey):** agave and maple.
- ✿ **Rice crackers:** add hummus, tomato and avocado.
- ✿ **Pasta, rice, noodles:** staples in my diet.
- ✿ **Pasta sauces:** of course!
- ✿ **Fortified cereal that's low in sugar and high in fibre:** fortified means it has added nutrients such as vitamin B 12, iron and calcium.

Fridge and freezer

- ✿ **Soy milk:** add to shakes and cereal. Did you know that a litre of cow's milk uses about 1050 litres of water to produce, while a litre of soy milk uses only 297 litres? Add oat, soy, coconut, almond and rice milks to your repertoire too.
- ✿ **Broccoli:** stir-fry with tofu, soy sauce and cashew nuts (a favourite of mine).
- ✿ **Hummus:** dollop it on pretty much anything. Add tahini, salad and pita bread and you have a whole meal.

- ✿ **Avocado:** smash on toast or squish into guacamole and add a sprinkle of seeds.
- ✿ **Mushrooms:** fry with onions, load onto potatoes. Delish!
- ✿ **Cauliflower:** roast in the oven and drizzle with tahini. Super easy.
- ✿ **Tofu:** grill with soy sauce on a hot pan. Good for stir-fries, curries and scrambled tofu.
- ✿ **Seitan:** perfect as a basis for a vegan bolognese sauce.
- ✿ **Nut-based margarine:** to spread on sandwiches.
- ✿ **Cashew cheeses:** crumble onto toast or pasta.
- ✿ **Spinach:** bake into a pie or pastry. Add pine nuts and cashew cheese for extra flavour.
- ✿ **Nut butters:** peanut, almond, cashew ... too good!
- ✿ **Coconut yoghurt:** add nuts and fruit or even a date or two.
- ✿ **Edamame:** sprinkle with a little salt.

Fact: The skins of fruits and vegetables often have a lot of dietary fibre, so don't peel them - simply wash and eat! A raw apple with skin has up to 332% more vitamin K, 142% more vitamin A, 115% more vitamin C, 20% more calcium and 19% more potassium than a peeled apple.

Go-to meals

New vegan recipe books are being published every week. I'm more of a make-it-up-as-I-go person in the kitchen, but if you want some direction you'll be spoilt for choice. Find your go-to, quick-and-easy recipes online – there are a billion and one, free and available; just hit Google!

I'm partial to a vegan spaghetti bolognaise. I first fry the onions and garlic, add fresh tomatoes, and then the frozen seitan mix. I mix in store-bought pasta sauce and herbs. My entire family loves it. My other fave is simply stir-frying tofu with olive oil and adding soy sauce. I put it on toast adding fresh tomatoes, vegan mayonnaise and avocado. Yum.

Melissa Hobbs of The Vegan Company says, 'My go-to is avocado on sourdough with lemon juice and chilli flakes. I also love rice with fried tofu, Asian greens, carrot, zucchini and a Japanese-style sauce; Thai curries; soups and Mexican. After watching *The Game Changers*, I've taken more interest in my food and have recently discovered fried cauliflower rice. So good!'[27]

> '**I always have tofu in the fridge and a burrito kit in the pantry for when I'm feeling lazy, and chia pudding is my crack.**'
>
> Tess Miller,
> Vegan A-Team

If you're looking for meal ideas, everything on the list below has been tried and tested by our Vegan A-Team:

- ✿ Baked vegies, like potato, beetroot and carrots, with tofu
- ✿ Baked sweet potato stuffed with black beans, garlic and onion
- ✿ Vegie stir-fries – add extra protein like tofu, nuts or mushrooms
- ✿ Scrambled tofu on toast
- ✿ Buddha bowls
- ✿ Vegie sushi
- ✿ Avocado on toast – sprinkle seeds and cherry tomatoes, tahini or cashew cheese
- ✿ Quinoa and toasted muesli bowl with banana, raisins and almond milk
- ✿ Steamed vegies with a big dollop of hummus
- ✿ Pasta with tomato and lentil sauce
- ✿ Spaghetti with vegan bolognese made from base of seitan or eggplant
- ✿ Falafel with hummus and tahini – eat with or without pita bread (and pickles are a must!)
- ✿ Tofu and mushroom curry
- ✿ Rice and quinoa burger with baked sweet potato
- ✿ Lentil and vegie soup with wholemeal pasta
- ✿ Salt and pepper tofu
- ✿ Three-bean chilli
- ✿ Green salad with beans, mushrooms and flavoured tofu
- ✿ Vegetable stew with tofu.

Baking

If you love to bake, it can seem tricky to replace eggs successfully. Depending on whether you're wanting to bind or to create moisture and whether your dish is sweet or savoury, here are some substitutions:

- ❀ **Applesauce:** adds moisture and flavour (cookies and breads).
- ❀ **Ground flax seed or chia seed plus 3 tablespoons of water:** good binding effects (burgers or muffins).
- ❀ **Mashed banana or avocado:** adds moisture and sweetness (cakes and brownies).
- ❀ **Pureed pumpkin, sweet potato or squash:** adds moisture and flavour (muffins and bread).
- ❀ **Silken tofu:** adds creamy texture (quiche).
- ❀ **Chickpea flour:** good for binding and raising (scones and cookies).
- ❀ **Creamy nut butter:** good for binding (cookies, pancakes and brownies).

Snacks

Having easy go-to snacks will help make the transition to vegan smoother. My current favourites include crackers and hummus, mixed nuts and dates.

Here are the top ideas from our Vegan A-Team:

- ❀ Crackers or fresh vegies with delicious spreads of hummus, tahini, or peanut or almond butter.

- ✿ Handful of mixed nuts and dried fruit for magnesium and healthy fats.
- ✿ Protein balls made from almond flour, seeds and dates.
- ✿ Dates stuffed with walnuts and/or bananas with walnuts (winning combos!).
- ✿ Kale chips and seaweed snacks.
- ✿ Rice crackers and cashew cheese.
- ✿ Coconut yoghurt with walnuts and blueberries or kiwifruit.
- ✿ Smoothies.

Smoothies

You can pack a lot of essential nutrients into a single smoothie! Many vegans swear by starting their morning with a smoothie that uses a mixture of ingredients that are rich in protein, calcium and iron.

Vegan breakfast smoothies are a huge trend on social media – you can find inspirational and beautiful pictures to help you discover your favourite combo. Throw in anything that's otherwise tricky to incorporate in your daily diet – we're talking flax seeds, chia, spinach, kale, dates, tahini ... you name it and you can drink it in a smoothie (almost!). Add a dollop of nut butter and some soy or almond milk, and Bob's your uncle! My personal favourite smoothie is made from soy milk, banana, date, almond butter, raw tahini and chia seeds. Katrina Fox, journalist and author, tells me she makes hers with orange, banana, strawberry, kale, chia and hemp seeds. Of course there are numerous vitamins, antioxidants and minerals not included in the list below and you can't go wrong with throwing in your favourite fruits and vegies, from carrots to peaches. (This is a drink, so remember to add a liquid too!)

What you need: a blender and a glass. Easy!

Add one or more of the below proteins:

- ✿ 1 cup unsweetened soy milk (7 grams protein)
- ✿ 1 cup unsweetened oat milk (3 grams protein)
- ✿ 1 cup unsweetened almond milk (2 grams protein)
- ✿ 1 cup raw canned coconut milk (4.57 grams protein)
- ✿ 1 tablespoon peanut or almond butter (7.1 grams or 6.7 grams protein)
- ✿ 1 cup raw chopped kale (3 grams protein)
- ✿ 1 large date (0.17 grams protein)
- ✿ 1 mango, cut up (2.8 grams protein)

Add one or more of the below calcium sources:

- ✿ 2 tablespoons of raw tahini (130 mg calcium)
- ✿ ½ cup kale (90 mg calcium)
- ✿ 1 tablespoon of chia seeds (75 mg calcium)
- ✿ 1 tablespoon of ground flax seeds (18 mg calcium)
- ✿ 2 tablespoons of raw wakame seaweed (15 mg calcium)

Add one or more of the below iron sources:

- ✿ ½ cup of frozen berries (0.14 mg iron)
- ✿ 1 tablespoon spirulina powder (2 mg iron)

- 🌸 2 tablespoons hemp seeds (1.59 mg iron)
- 🌸 ½ cup rolled oats soaked overnight (1.7 mg iron)
- 🌸 1 cup raw spinach (0.86 mg iron)

Blend together, pour into a tall glass, then enjoy!

Soy – mistaken identity

Poor soybeans; they should sue for misrepresentation! As someone who likes a good soy latte, I'm often asked, 'But aren't you contributing to environmental destruction?' In reality, 80 per cent of soybeans grown in the world are fed to farmed animals, not humans. If we stopped eating animals, we'd reduce the huge tracts of land used to grow soy. Soy milk and tofu are not the culprit; beef is.

Soy is also often associated with negative health effects, but the science is questionable (with many articles rumoured to be funded by the dairy industry!). Soy is, in fact, healthy and studies have shown that when it comes to breast cancer, soy milk can reduce the risk, increase lifespan after a diagnosis, and reduce the recurrence of the disease. Soy has no adverse effects on the thyroid gland, but note that it may reduce the absorption of thyroid medications.[28] For men, studies show it has no adverse effects, only positive, as soy reduces the risk of prostate cancer.[29]

Cheese addiction

Many of us find the most
challenging part of becoming vegan
is saying goodbye to cheese. It's no
coincidence we're all so addicted.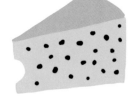
Cheese contains casein and casein fragments called
casomorphins, which are a morphine-like compound.

These opiate molecules are a natural component of dairy
products like cheese and yoghurt, and a major reason why
dairy products can be so moreish. As Dr Neal Barnard
explains, when we eat dairy, the opiates 'attach to the
same brain receptors as heroin and morphine. They are not
strong enough to get you arrested, but they are just strong
enough to keep you coming back for more.'[30]

Some researchers believe this addictive effect occurs for
evolutionary reasons to ensure babies (humans, cows and
so on) continue to nurse during infancy, which helps the
survival of the species. That helps to explain why babies look
so blissed out when breastfeeding, and why it feels so good
to eat cheese. A cup of milk contains 7.7 grams of protein,
80 per cent of which is casein. In a supermarket packet
of 350 grams of cheddar cheese, the protein increases to
about 87 grams and so does the morphine-like compound.

Our brain's 'reward centre' releases dopamine when we
eat cheese, just like it does with other addictive drugs. This
explains why it's so delicious, why it causes cravings and
why we have a hard time giving it up.

DIFFERENT STAGES OF LIFE

If you have questions or concerns about your or your family's health, it's a good idea to see a doctor or health professional who has experience with vegan diets. Here are some tips to get you started.

Growing bodies

- ✿ **Calcium:** This strengthens bones and is important during adolescence when our bodies are growing. We reach our maximum bone density during teenagehood and then it gets less and less as we get older. Our calcium requirements depend on our age: 1300 mg/day for 12- to 18-year-olds; 1000 mg for 9- to 11-year-olds; 700 mg for 4- to 8-year-olds.[31]

- ✿ **B12:** When you're young and growing, your developing brain must have its daily B12. Keep your B12 drops or pills near your breakfast spot and be sure you don't forget to take them!

- ✿ **Omega 3s:** These fatty acids are good for mood, brain power, learning and concentration. If you have bumpy dry skin on your upper outer arms or find it hard to focus on schoolwork, a lack of Omega 3 may be the culprit. Linseeds, chia and walnuts are great sources of Omega 3. As mentioned earlier, not everyone's body can convert them efficiently. You may want to take an Omega 3 supplement that's made from a non-toxic algae oil and contains DHA and EPA.

- ✿ **Protein:** Young people can increase their protein intake during growth spurts. But generally, protein isn't a concern for any age in particular and too much can actually strain our kidneys and liver.

✿ ***Tip for vegan teens:*** Eat vegetables! Don't only eat a vegan version of your friends' junk-food diet, but rather boost your health and energy with vegies, legumes and wholefoods packed with micronutrients. And remember, exercise builds healthy bones too.

Pregnancy

Eating a healthy diet is more important than ever when growing one or more bubs. A healthy well-balanced vegan diet is considered by medical experts safe for pregnancy. However, you may want to consider, with the help of a dietician, creating a special eating plan so you have the confidence you're getting everything you and your baby need. This is especially true if you're suffering from any health complications or a high-risk pregnancy.

In addition to the usual pregnancy advice (such as taking daily folic acid and prenatal supplements), here are a few general points for vegan pregnant women to keep in mind:

1. A daily B12 supplement is very important as the growing fetus requires freshly absorbed B12. Speak to your health professional about other supplements such as folic acid, iron, iodine, vitamin D and DHA (Omega 3).

2. You need about twice as much iron as normal because your body uses it to make extra blood. You'll need about 27 mg per day and can get iron through foods such as lentils, chickpeas, tofu, cashew nuts, chia seeds, kale, quinoa and fortified breakfast cereals. Increasing vitamin C can help your body absorb iron. Look to add food such as broccoli, oranges and kiwifruit. Let your doctor know about your vegan diet so they can monitor your iron and haemoglobin levels.

3. Calcium helps your bones stay strong and promotes your baby's bone growth. You need about 1000 mg/day when pregnant. Calcium-fortified foods and drinks, as well as figs and almonds, are all good sources.

4. Be mindful you're getting enough plant-based proteins (like legumes) in your meals or smoothies. Pregnant women need something in the ball-park of 70 grams per day.[32] A protein-packed day's meal plan could look like this: breakfast of oatmeal with fruit, walnuts and chia seeds. A lunch of lentil soup and a hummus

sandwich. A slice of wholewheat bread and nut butter for a snack, and a bowl of rice, almonds and chickpeas for dinner.

Breastfeeding

To make great-quality breast milk for a new little sweetie-pie, women should:

1. Eat more calories. You'll need about 1000 more calories every day in the first six months.
2. Keep your protein levels high, just like when you're pregnant.
3. Up your calcium. Breastfeeding mums generally need about 1250 mg/day or 80% more calcium than normal.
4. Be sure you have at least 9 mg iron daily.
5. You need to keep your daily B12 supplement going – this is important also for the baby's brain development.
6. Continue with your high-quality multivitamin that contains iodine, vitamin D and zinc.
7. Don't forget your Omega 3 supplement made from algae oil with EPA and DHA.
8. Keep hydrated!

Perimenopause

There is a huge amount of debate around the topic of the onset of menopause, aka perimenopause, and what causes or helps women get through the various potential ailments associated with it, such as anxiety, depression, irritability, and poor memory and concentration.

However, there's no indication a vegan diet has any negative effects. On the contrary, many doctors believe a diet high in animal fats can negatively impact hormones and contribute to perimenopausal problems.[33]

To reduce the impacts of perimenopause, vegans can try eating fewer refined carbs and sugars (skip those donuts!), instead adding whole grains, nuts, seeds, essential fats and fresh fruit and vegies. Adding plant oestrogens (phytoestrogens) like unprocessed soya beans (edamame), miso soup, or soya flour is also proven to help with hot flushes. Women going through menopause are also recommended to up their protein. If you're over 50, rather than 0.8g/kg the number increases to about 1–1.2g/kg of body weight.[34]

Post-menopause

Osteoporosis, or a thinning of the bone tissue, can be common in menopausal women. It is caused by numerous factors, including genetics, lifestyle and diet. Research into the optimal amount of calcium is not conclusive, but the recommended amount for adults ranges from 400–800 mg. Our bodies absorb calcium from vegies just as well as from milk – sometimes better![35] The healthiest sources of vegan calcium are greens and beans like pinto, black-eyed and navy. Green leafy vegetables are also loaded with calcium. Spinach has a lot of calcium, but it's hard for our bodies to absorb it. A varied diet of beans, lentils, legumes and vegies will give you everything you need.

Other calcium-rich foods include:

1. **Calcium-set tofu:** 100 grams = 350 mg calcium
2. **Dark leafy greens:** collard, turnip greens, spinach and kale, 1 cup boiled = 170–270 mg calcium
3. **Orange juice:** 1 cup calcium-fortified = 350 mg calcium
4. **Tofu:** ½ cup = 258 mg calcium
5. **Fortified plant milk:** 200 ml = 240 mg calcium
6. **Oatmeal:** 1 cup of instant = 215 mg calcium
7. **Soybeans:** (edamame) 1 cup boiled = 175 mg calcium
8. **Vegetarian baked beans:** 1 cup = 127 mg calcium
9. **Broccoli:** 1 cup boiled from frozen = 94 mg calcium
10. **Dried figs:** 10 medium = 269 mg calcium
11. **Almonds:** 30 g = 72 mg calcium
12. **Chia seeds:** 1 tablespoon = 69 mg calcium

Vegan families

How each family member approaches veganism is a highly individual choice and, of course, dependent on their age, stage and personality. Some vegans go it solo, preparing their own meals while others in the family eat non-vegan food. Others slowly inch forward towards the goal of a vegan home, attempting to get all members of the household on board. And then there are those inspirational individuals who manage to raise their families vegan from the get-go.

I have done a mixture of the above list, endlessly guilt-ridden about buying non-vegan food for my family, and berating myself because I feel I'm not doing enough. I have raised my daughter, Jasmine, who is now 15 years old, as a pescatarian. She has never tasted meat or shown interest in trying it. While she's not vegan (yet!), as she's grown older, she's decided to replace some animal products with alternatives, such as plant-based milk in her morning bran cereal. I've tried to nudge the rest of my family down the vegan road. My twin boys now enjoy soy yoghurts, vegan meatballs and bolognese, and my husband has replaced the cow's milk in his latte and recently announced he would give up fish. Slowly but surely.

Zoe Borbiro is one of the amazing people who has done the whole enchilada and raised three healthy vegan kids. She says:

'The highs of raising vegan kids are seeing my children experiencing life differently. Along with animals' intrinsic value and rights, they see that what may be normal to others may not necessarily be the only way to act and think. My children are critical and empathic thinkers. They are self-assured and have integrity due to thinking and acting outside of the norm; they know the value of speaking up for and educating others where possible. The challenges as a vegan parent are watching my kids learning to be different from their peers and sometimes singled out when they are young.

Watching my kids answering sometimes inappropriate questions from adults who feel confronted and conflicted by a child whose ethics can make them see their own hypocrisy can be challenging – and also pride-invoking when hearing my children's responses. Explaining to young children why some people think it's okay to pay others to breed, harm and kill animals unnecessarily can be heartbreaking at first, though it does help vegan children manage by learning that people can and do change, especially when they see children thriving as vegans. As my kids get older these challenges have certainly solidified their ethics but in the early years it can be frustrating and emotionally exhausting for them and me.'

Zoe has been relaxed about counting grams of iron and calcium, taking the same easygoing approach as I tend to do.

'We haven't focused on health too much. We eat pretty simple food, indulge whenever we want, and take B12. The kids have had occasional blood tests since they were about 10 and the results have always been great.'

SPECIAL DIETS

It's important to work with an experienced dietician if you have any health concerns, allergies or issues. Eating lots of different kinds of whole plant foods, including whole grains, legumes, nuts and seeds, and vegetables and fruits can be good for our gut health. But take it slowly. The microbiome in our gut – trillions of healthy bacteria, fungi and other microbes that control our digestion – may need to get used to the new plant-based foods we add to our diet. Every time we eat something, there are specific bacteria that help us digest it; if we're used to eating lots of legumes, we will have plenty of bacteria in our gut that thrive on legumes and help to digest them. If legumes have never been our thing in the past, we will likely lack that specific bacteria, so start with small amounts of new foods to slowly increase the bacteria you need.

You may want to receive personalised information as well as menu ideas if you have food restrictions or digestive issues. For example, if you have IBS (irritable bowel syndrome) or require a low-FODMAP diet, you may be wary of certain plant-based ingredients such as lentils, beans or chickpeas. You can look at creating a healthy daily meal plan with lower FODMAP foods such as potatoes, spinach, hummus, tofu, quinoa, rice, carrots, tomatoes, gluten-free bread, peanut butter, banana, rolled oats and almond milk. There are also specialised recipe books focusing on low-FODMAP vegan cooking. If you're struggling, remember: don't let perfect be the enemy of good. Any reduction in our consumption of animal products is a win for animals, the climate and our Earth.

BHAVANI BAUMANN

Bhavani is the co-founder of the first vegan pub in Australia, The Green Lion. She's been vegan for four years and vegetarian since birth.

WHY I MADE THE SWITCH FROM VEGETARIANISM TO VEGANISM

I was reading an article about dairy farming when I realised it was no different to eating meat due to the treatment of the cows and the baby boy calves being killed. My husband was making pizza and I yelled out, 'I don't want cheese on my pizza!' and I never looked back. My inspiration for going vegan is about compassion for all living beings. I don't want to be responsible for any harm to anyone.

MY BELIEF

All living beings are equal and we should all have a right to a full life.

MY ADVICE FOR COOKING VEGAN FOOD

Keep it simple. Often people think cooking vegan food is somehow more complicated or time-consuming. The easiest thing for a new vegan to do is to simply substitute the animal products in your meal with vegan equivalents – which are available in most major supermarkets.

TIPS ON TURNING YOUR FAVOURITE MEALS VEGAN

To make your favourite lasagne, simply switch the beef mince for soy mince and a vegan béchamel; there are lots of good recipes online. Besides that, just make sure your pasta sheets are egg-free. Napolitano sauce is usually vegan.

Grab some vegan sausages from the supermarket and puff pastry. This makes fantastic sausage-roll finger food for parties and I've never had one person notice the difference.

Egg replacer is available in most supermarkets and is great for all your baking needs. Make sure you follow the instructions on the packet and the result is identical to using eggs.

WHAT'S THE MOST IMPORTANT THING TO REMEMBER?

Be kind to yourself. This is a deeply personal journey. Ask questions, seek help when needed and go out and eat in different vegan restaurants to really understand how diverse cruelty-free eating can be.

4

FASHION, LIFESTYLE & ADVOCACY

'Living cruelty-free isn't just keeping animals off plates. Fashion plays an instrumental part in ensuring the term "cruelty-free" extends to all corners of one's lifestyle.'

ANNA WEATHERLAKE

VOICELESS AMBASSADOR

Beginning a vegan journey is a holistic experience, a path towards a kinder, more compassionate, and non-violent life. Food is the obvious starting point, but clothes, make-up, entertainment and even pets come into play as part of a vegan lifestyle. The information here is to help you learn. Take your time if you need to, because the tortoise wins the race, not the hare.

'UNLESS SOMEONE LIKE YOU CARES A WHOLE AWFUL LOT, NOTHING IS GOING TO GET BETTER. IT'S NOT.'

DR SEUSS

FASHION

The fashion industry is one of the worst offenders in terms of animal cruelty, and often when we begin the vegan journey we start to become mindful of what we wear. The great news is that fashion designers and brands are exploding with new vegan-friendly products.

Celebrities with powerful reaches are enthusiastically launching new lines on an almost weekly basis, mainstreaming vegan fashion like never before.

Los Angeles hosts Vegan Fashion Week and the world's most famous designers, including Coco Chanel, Versace, Gucci, Burberry and Giorgio Armani, are stopping their use of fur. Miley Cyrus opened her own vegan fashion line, saying, 'I am so excited ... to show to the world that we don't have to torture animals to look fabulous.' The Beastie Boys collaborated with Adidas to start a vegan shoe.[1] The vegan-friendly celeb list is long. Even Kim Kardashian West has got on board the fur-free train, posting to her 146 million followers that she's now only using faux fur. Celebrated Australian designer Akira Isogawa told Voiceless, 'I think we have to take responsibility for whatever we do. I have abandoned the idea of using skins, furs. I think that is an obvious choice. And I also let the world know that choice professionally.'[2]

All these new vegan-friendly labels and brands now make it fun to go shopping. Diddy Mymin from our A-Team says, 'Vegan fashion has become a hobby for me. I love finding great vegan shoes and bags. Being vegan does not mean you have to dress badly at all. There are great alternatives!'

Tess Miller, another A-Team member, gets active online:

'My smartphone is king when it comes to finding vegan fashion, beauty and household products. Find groups, pages or influencers that share your values and tastes. Download apps to help you check what's what – you get very good at knowing which of these to search and when.'

Vegans often find themselves on a spectrum in the world of fashion. Broadly speaking, most won't wear leather, fur or skins. However, there are some people who do continue purchasing wool, silk or cashmere, even though they are animal products. It's up to you where and how to start. I personally suggest beginning with leather.

LEATHER

Leather is processed animal skin made from cows and calves, but it can also come from kangaroos, goats, pigs, deer, reptiles, crocodiles, ostriches and even dogs. The global leather market is worth over $300 billion, making leather a massive industry in its own right.[3] This means it cannot be justified as simply a 'by-product' (a secondary product that's made while making something else) of the meat and dairy industry; rather, it is an extremely lucrative 'co-product' (something that's produced jointly with another product).

The meat industry and the leather industry can't be separated. For someone who wants to forgo beef for the sake of animal protection or out of concern for the unfolding climate crisis and the destruction of the environment, abstaining from leather is part of this too.

Leather is sourced from our production of billions of cattle, requiring massive swathes of our Earth's land. Cattle are responsible for huge environmental destruction in Australia and around the world; cattle farming is considered to have destroyed 79.5 per cent of Brazil's Amazon region. Demand for leather fuels the destruction of the Amazon, not just as a by-product of beef. Social justice issues intersect here too – sadly, cattle ranching in the Amazon uses most of Brazil's slave labour.[4]

The environmental issues caused by leather don't end there. During the tanning process, massive amounts of toxic chromium pollute our waterways, placing leather tanning as number five on the world's top ten worst toxic pollution problems.[5] Chromium causes enormous health issues, often in developing countries where there is less access to clean water.

Leather equals cows, and we know how the welfare of cows is compromised in the beef industry. According to reports, cows for beef production frequently suffer from heat and cold stress. Their respiratory system becomes diseased due to overcrowding and inadequate ventilation. Beef cattle are generally not diagnosed or treated for illnesses in a timely fashion, and their digestive systems struggle from their unnatural diet of intensive concentrate feeding. They develop behavioural disorders because of lack of space and being forced to unnaturally co-mingle in crowded feedlots.[6]

In Australia, leather is often imported from India and China, two of the largest producers of cow leather. Investigations have revealed major welfare issues in the Indian leather supply-chain, where exhausted animals are 'encouraged' to keep moving by workers who break the cows' tails and rub chilli peppers into their eyes. In China, animals used in the leather industry are even less protected than in countries like Australia and the United States and in the European Union, as China lacks any national animal welfare legislation.

If protecting dogs from suffering touches your heart more than protecting cows, consider this: over two million cats and dogs are killed for their skins in China every year, in horrific circumstances. Companies intentionally mislabel dog and cat skins as 'leather', or don't accurately label their place of origin, knowing that consumers wouldn't want to buy and wear part of a dog or cat. Sometimes we can buy something that looks like leather, when it is, in fact, dog skin from China.

Local Australian leather comes from animals in the dairy and meat industries. This means that buying leather supports numerous cruel practices in Australia's dairy industry, such as the endless cycle of pregnancy, birth and high-intensity milking, which can cause lameness and mastitis, as well as mutilations like tail docking, disbudding and dehorning without pain relief. And, as we talked about in Chapter 2, newborn male 'bobby' calves are routinely transported to slaughter at a few days old, considered 'waste products' to the industry.

Losing leather from your closet may feel like a lot because leather is everywhere – bags, shoes, insoles, linings and more. It's worth always checking seemingly non-leather products too: I recently found a gorgeous brand of recycled 'eco-purses' but, investigating closely as I'm inclined to do after years of experience, I noticed the edging of the zipper was made of leather. Don't fear. The pleasure of not purchasing leather, knowing you're doing a good thing, outweighs any inconvenience!

Alternatives

Fake leather has been around for almost a century, and I've worn many variations myself for the last 20 years – saving me a ton of money on shoes.

It's better to buy less and pay more. We know now that 'fast fashion' is not only contributing to animal abuse but also overloading our landfills, polluting waterways with harsh chemicals and trapping women in poverty.[7]

Cheap synthetic 'leather' can be made from polyurethane (also known as PU or PUR), which is not good for the environment. If we want to tick all the good-citizen boxes, the answers to our problems are eco-friendly, sustainable vegan fabrics, which are now, lucky for us, blossoming as an industry. These ingenious materials are made from paper, cork, recycled rubber, plastic bottles, tyres and even mushrooms, coconuts, oranges, apples and pineapples. Here are a few examples:

- ❀ **Recycled rubber and tyres:** Rubber used to be naturally derived from the Pará rubber tree, but today it is often made from petroleum. Rubber is used everywhere, from tyres to fire hoses, and disposing of this material is extremely polluting, with heavy metals and chemicals leaching into the soil and water systems. Many designers have found a second life for recycled rubber, replicating the texture and density of leather to make handbags, shoes and belts.
- ❀ **Waxed cotton:** While this method has long been used for jeans, organic waxed cotton is now

recognised as an eco-friendly and vegan alternative to leather. It's pliable and waterproof, just like leather, with the added bonus of being machine washable, which means avoiding the harsh dry-cleaning chemicals usually needed for leather.

- ✿ **Fruit waste:** Many new wearable materials are being derived from fruit and vegetable waste like orange skins and banana peels. One brand is transforming apple fibres into beautiful bags while another creates 'leather' from the waste parts of the pineapple bush. Not only are these natural and sustainable alternatives to leather, they also help provide additional income for local farmers and reduce waste, making this trend an all-around ethical gem.
- ✿ **K-leather:** Most people have never heard of K-leather, but if you check the small print you'll discover it's made from Australia's national symbol and beloved native animal, the kangaroo.

The commercial killing of kangaroos is a multi-million dollar industry and the largest slaughter of land-based wildlife on Earth.[8] Over 90 million kangaroos and wallabies have been killed for their meat and skins over the last 30 years in Australia. There are four species of kangaroo and two wallaby species that are killed commercially. Most skins are produced as a co-product of the commercial kangaroo industry and exported across the world for use in everything from clothing to car upholstery.

Contrary to popular misconception, kangaroos are not farmed – they are shot in the wild. The industry originally started based on a belief that kangaroo populations were exploding and that they were a 'pest' for farmers, competing with their sheep and cattle for grasses. The scientific evidence for these claims is now being hotly debated. A National Code of Practice[9] is supposed to mitigate kangaroo suffering, but it is practically ineffective due to the fact that the killing occurs at night in remote locations across Australia's vast landscape. Although shooters are required to secure a head shot, this is not achieved all the time, and there is no independent oversight or supervision. Non-fatal body shots are an inevitable part of the industry, causing painful injuries, prolonged suffering and a slow death for hunted kangaroos.[10] As a former kangaroo shooter explains:

'The mouth of a kangaroo can be blown off and the kangaroo can escape to die of shock and starvation. Forearms can be blown off, as can ears, eyes and noses. Stomachs can be hit, expelling the contents with the kangaroo still alive. Backbones can be pulverised to an unrecognisable state etc. Hind legs can be shattered with the kangaroo desperately trying to get away on the other or without the use of either. To deny that this goes on is just an exercise in attempting to fool the public.'[11]

Mothers and their babies, called joeys, form close bonds and communicate with each other using unique calls, and mothers and daughters maintain long-term connections. Eastern grey and western grey kangaroos are particularly social animals who live in large groups called 'mobs'. Their social structure is decimated by the commercial kill.

Despite the known cruelties to joeys, it is legal for shooters to kill female kangaroos with dependent young. These pouch babies are considered wastage for the industry and thrown away. The older joeys, who live outside their mother's pouches and are not killed immediately, will likely die as a result of starvation, exposure or predation without their mothers to teach them vital survival skills, such as finding food, water and shelter.

Fact: **Females kangas can choose if they want a boy or girl baby, and if there's a drought they can even pause their pregnancy until the weather improves.**

FUR

Fur is a $40-billion industry and, despite a significant swing in public opinion against fur in the 1990s, today there are more fashion designers than ever using fur. You might not see a fur coat like in days of old, but fur is prevalent in ready-to-wear lines.

Most fur comes from animals in 'farms'. One hundred million animals are bred and killed in these intensive systems including minks, dogs, rabbits, foxes, sables and chinchillas. There are fur farms throughout the world, with major suppliers in Europe, the United States, Canada and China.

The animals are usually confined in small, barren wire cages where they are stressed and unable to perform basic behaviours. Abnormal behaviours such as fur-chewing, cage-circling and self-harm then result.

The furry mink is the most popular animal for breeding and killing. Minks are beautiful animals – their extraordinarily silky, soft, glossy fur has caused their downfall.

In nature, minks are predators and semi-aquatic, born to hunt and swim. They love eating frogs and hanging around the banks of wetlands, lakes, rivers and streams. They don't like to spend time with others and have large territories where they enjoy their own company (introverts rejoice!). Obviously in mink farms they can't swim or do any of their natural activities. Rather, they can often be seen pacing and circling repetitively, signs of mental stress and suffering.

Farming isn't the only cruelty inflicted on fur animals; both the trapping of wild animals and the slaughter of animals in the fur industry cause horrific pain and misery.

Trapping

About 15 per cent of fur comes from animals caught in the wild with traps; the animals often suffer painful and prolonged deaths. Even though steel-jawed traps are banned in numerous countries and jurisdictions, they continue to be used in some places. By clamping down on the captured animal's limb, they cause significant injuries, both through the steel clamp itself and the animal's reaction to being trapped (such as self-mutilation caused by attempting escape). The traps capture a range of animals, not just the intended targets, with animals often left to suffer for extended periods of time until the hunter arrives to kill them. Leg-hold traps are considered to be more 'humane' as rubber padding provides protection from the steel jaws. However, even these cause fear and distress for the animal for sometimes as long as 24 hours.

Slaughter

Slaughter methods in the fur industry (carbon monoxide gassing, electrocution and neck-breaking) can also end up being crueller than those in the meat industry because the fur needs to be protected from damage. In some countries such as China there are reports of animals being skinned alive and other horrific acts during slaughter.[12]

Because of the known cruelty and suffering, many countries and jurisdictions around the world have banned the production, importation and sale of fur. But there is still a long, long way to go.

ᴡᴏᴏʟ

Sheep are commonly believed to be docile, gentle and not so smart. But recent scientific research has discovered that the humble sheep is way more complex than we imagined. They each have distinct personalities — similar to humans; some are bold and gregarious while others are shy. Their emotions are complex with strong mother–baby bonds and social groupings that go beyond their need for food. They can recognise each other's faces.[13]

Sheep farmed for their wool experience many procedures with no pain relief. This includes castration and cutting off their long tails. Mulesing involves cutting off a large piece of flesh near a sheep's breech (or backside) to avoid blowflies nesting in the folds of skin. Lambs are restrained while their backsides are cut with a knife or blade. They can experience days of pain before their wounds heal.[14]

Mulesing, despite the public outcry and promises from the wool industry to address the welfare issue, still requires no mandatory pain relief. About 30 million lambs are mulesed every year in Australia, while New Zealand has banned the practice entirely, making it a criminal offence.

Some Australian and international brands are now refusing to purchase wool from mulesed sheep because of the inherent cruelty, creating a growing market of wool from non-mulesed sheep, which sells at a premium.

OTHER CREATURES

Numerous animals have their fur, feathers and skin taken for fashion. Sometimes it's easy to forget these materials actually involve hurting, harming or killing an animal. Try to swap your mohair (angora goats), angora (angora rabbits), silk (silkworm cocoons) and cashmere (Kashmir goats) for sustainable, ethical vegan alternatives. Grace Prael from the Vegan A-Team recommends: 'Check the materials tag. Look out for things such as leather, suede, silk, angora, cashmere, fur trims, feather (down) filling in winter jackets and wool.'

Duck or geese feathers (down), for example, are sourced for our jackets, pillows and blankets. Feathers are either stripped off once the ducks have been killed, or plucked out, handfuls at a time, while the bird is still alive. Gemma Davis, from the Compassionate Road website, writes, 'It's the equivalent of someone ripping the hair off your head. In chunks. Without your permission while you are fully conscious, legs bound.' China is the largest producer of down, and its methods are not very transparent. Countless investigations show feathers being taken off live ducks.

SECOND-HAND FASHION

Sometimes purchasing second-hand fashion is the most ethical and environmentally sustainable decision we can make. As A-Team member Kylie Walsh says, 'I prefer to buy my clothes second-hand; not everything is vegan, but it does give items a second life.' Some vegans feel that wearing their grandmother's vintage fur coat or buying second-hand fur and skins is okay. But many people, including me, believe it sends the wrong message. Wearing real skins makes them look socially acceptable. Instead, I like to model new plant-based materials and products that help these innovative businesses grow and prosper.

SHAUN MOSS

Shaun is a qualified personal trainer and follows a clean, whole-food vegan diet.

HOW I BEGAN

I felt guilty about eating food that required extreme cruelty to produce when I didn't really need to. I was vegetarian for 14 years. Later, I learned that producing dairy products, eggs and honey involved cruelty as well, so I cut those. I also learned about the adverse environmental and health impacts of animal products. But the primary initial reason was that I couldn't in good conscience be complicit in cruelty to animals.

DISCUSSING VEGANISM WITH OTHERS

Be gentle when you talk to others. Many of us were once non-vegans. Although intelligent, we didn't know we were doing anything wrong, and we didn't like it when people told us what to do. I'm being honest when I say that becoming vegan is the best thing I've ever done, and this gets people interested. I'm also not afraid to say that eating animal-based foods is killing our most valuable resource – the biosphere – is horribly cruel, and has been proven to be unhealthy. I also suggest making sure you look good by eating right, training hard and getting into shape. Encourage people to just try being vegan for a month (for example, by participating in Veganuary or No Meat May or doing a 30-day challenge or whatever) and see how they feel.

MY GO-TO MEALS

Paleo muesli with nut milk. Fruit. Nuts. Soups, curries or salads with tofu or tempeh. Burrito bowls without rice. Because I lift weights, I also have about 160 grams of plant-based protein powder a day.

HOW TO NOT FEEL 'DEPRIVED'

If you're deeply missing some favourite foods, they're available in vegan form, so learn where to find them or how to make them. Then if you get a craving for a burger or ice-cream or cheese sandwich, you can have it.

Beauty

Being beautiful is not about what's on the outside, but what we grow and nurture within. And, for me, the most gorgeous thing a human being can possess is a kind heart. That's why living a compassionate lifestyle, in all senses of the word, is a beauty must. There is no need to test our make-up, shampoo or other beauty products on animals. Make sure the brand you love has zero tolerance for cosmetic testing or switch over to one of the many that do care about animals.

The world of beauty can be a little confusing, but there are two labels or symbols to keep any eye out for: one is 'cruelty-free' and the other is 'vegan'. Cruelty-free means the company does not test their products on animals and none of their ingredients are produced with animal-testing either. But, the product may still contain animal products. Vegan means there are no animal products in the ingredients but (although this should be an obvious part of a vegan philosophy) it doesn't guarantee there has been no animal testing. Of course, the best products are both vegan and cruelty-free, which is still a small but growing market.

You might be wondering why vegan beauty products are needed. Well, most of us have no idea that there are a range of hidden animal parts in our everyday beauty items.

Here's a selection of ingredients to watch out for:

- ❀ **Carmine:** a red dye derived from crushed female cochineal scale insects, commonly used in lipsticks, blushes and eyeshadows.
- ❀ **Snail mucin:** an extract from the slime of snails, often used in skincare products.
- ❀ **Keratin:** a protein derived from the ground horns, hooves, claws, nails, hair, scales and feathers of diverse vertebrates and used in skincare and haircare products. Collagen and elastin are other animal-derived proteins used in skincare.
- ❀ **Milk products:** often used as a skin and hair conditioner.
- ❀ **Guanine:** the part of fish scales used in nail polish for a pearlescent pigment.
- ❀ **Lanolin:** the secretion of the sebaceous glands of sheep. This is washed out of the wool of shorn or slaughtered sheep and purified.
- ❀ **Bee products:** including beeswax, honey, propolis, bee pollen and royal jelly.
- ❀ **Animal hair:** used for make-up brushes, hairbrushes and shaving brushes.

It may feel a little overwhelming to immediately start using only products that are cruelty-free *and* vegan, so some people prioritise one over the other at the start – you might find this a good approach to begin with. As much as possible, our aim is to support ethical companies and shun unkind ones with our precious dollar. This tactic has worked well in the USA with recent hashtags like #GrabYourWallet.

Certain brands perceived as unethical have been boycotted, causing their stock price to drop significantly.

Companies care about what consumers demand and respond accordingly. They know they need to keep us happy when they see research like this – two thirds of Americans take part in at least one boycott a year, and 75 per cent of the USA's 80 million millennials, with $200 billion of annual buying power, say it's important to them that a company gives back to society. The current rise in conscious consumerism led to 2018 being dubbed 'The Year of the Influential Sustainable Consumer'.

But consumer activism isn't new. The Free Produce Movement in the 1840s boycotted goods made by enslaved people, such as cotton. Never underestimate the power of your wallet to create change!

As with many aspects of veganism, celebrities are quickly becoming the biggest ambassadors. Their influence on society, politics and even legislation can't be underestimated. Via television and social media, celebs have a megaphone that can reach the ears of tens or hundreds of millions of people. And like us, many of them care deeply about animal-cruelty issues, have concerns about our environment, are worried about the climate crisis and want their voices heard. Lady Gaga launched a vegan and cruelty-free make-up line with the tagline, 'Cruelty-free and vegan. Because we love animals and you'. TV star Millie Bobby Brown has done the same with her products focusing on teenagers, Florence by Mills.

'A GO-TO ONLINE SEARCH IS: DOES [BRAND] TEST ON ANIMALS? ANOTHER I USE: IS [BRAND] VEGAN?'

—

GRACE PRAEL,
A-TEAM

Entertainment

An ethical approach towards animals spreads magic into all aspects of our lives. We now see the world through the lens of 'Is it kind to animals?' Using animals in and for entertainment is usually an exercise in *unkindness*. These industries include zoos and marine parks, racing (horse, greyhound), circuses, rodeos and fighting (roosters, bulls, dogs).

ZOOS AND MARINE PARKS

Zoos and marine parks are, in many ways, the most frustrating as they market themselves as a place for animal lovers. Really, they're the opposite. Part of a multibillion-dollar global industry, they are for-profit companies (unlike conservation or animal protection organisations, which are non-profit charities) with the primary aim of making money.

Rather than educating us about wildlife, permanently confining healthy animals in zoos and marine parks teaches our children lessons in disrespect. Millions of land and marine animals are caged, isolated, removed from their social groups and restrained from their natural behaviours. We may see animals up close, but what meaningful lessons do we learn? Often we leave with a distorted or inaccurate perception and the belief that we humans have every right to strip an animal's life of everything meaningful purely for our viewing pleasure.

While enclosures may look 'natural' with murals, moats and landscaping, it is not possible for an artificial environment to recreate the complexity and breadth of an animal's natural home. Unable to freely fly, run, hunt, climb, scavenge, forage, dig, explore and mate, animals are doomed to a life of permanent confinement, deprived of normal social interactions and often bored and lonely. For example, dolphins have complex systems of communication and strong relationships, including friends and maternity pods. They navigate their ocean environment and find food using sound waves or echolocation, something impossible to replicate in a marine park. 'Zoochosis' describes the abnormal, obsessive and repetitive behaviour seen in zoo animals, such as pacing, swaying, rocking, biting bars or biting themselves and other self-harming actions. Zoochosis is seen among tigers, lions, chimpanzees and other species kept in zoos.

Conservation can be used as a justification for the existence of zoos and marine parks but this is often 'greenwashing' (when a company conveys a false impression or exaggerates claims about helping the environment). Zoos and marine parks invest enormous resources into advertising and promotion. Yes, some do conservation work, but research has found the work is often inadequate. Conservation is a side-job to ticket sales, and investigations of zoos have found they contribute little to species conservation or public education, with their claims exaggerated, ambiguous and in some cases entirely unjustified. In essence, conservation cannot justify the keeping and breeding of wild animals in permanent captivity. These animals are for public display and entertainment, not species protection; very few will ever be returned to the wild. They stand like living museum pieces, symbols of how humans have destroyed our natural world.

There is no logical reason to keep wild animals in captivity when conservationists are able to study and protect animals in their natural habitats, ensuring their survival for generations.

Instead of going to a zoo or marine park, support one of the numerous charities that work to protect wild animals by conserving their natural habitats, ending poaching and stopping the wildlife trade. Or donate to sanctuaries that rescue, rehabilitate and release wild animals. If you want to see wild animals up close, visit sanctuaries that provide a home for injured or orphaned wild animals who are unable to be returned to the wild, or venture out into nature yourself. If possible, save up for your dream trip to Africa, Antarctica or Alaska and see animals living their best life: wild and free.

HORSE AND GREYHOUND RACING

Racing animals are bred for the purpose of profit. Once their financial value has diminished, through injury or loss of speed, they are promptly killed, often in horrific circumstance as recent exposés have shown.

Horses may suffer from torn ligaments and tendons, dislocated joints, fractures and pulmonary haemorrhages due to exertion. They tend to be confined for long periods in small stables, fed diets with high grain concentration (which can lead to ulcers), have their tongues tied by rubber bands[15] and are whipped repetitively. They can be shot on race day or at the end of their 'use' are killed for pet meat. Footage of racehorses being slaughtered (taken by animal activists) in 2019 was so appallingly cruel it led to calls for criminal charges against the abattoir. In Australia, where the Melbourne Cup horse race is traditionally watched live on TV by millions of people, there is a growing #nuptothecup movement, which is taking the sparkle out of the lucrative and powerful racing industry.

Greyhounds' welfare is equally endangered. These gentle dogs are subjected to social deprivation, inadequate housing, have a high rate of injury, suffer from heat- stress-related injury and physical over-exertion leading to seizures. Many collapse post-race. They are drugged to increase performance, and live baiting (using live animals on the racetrack to encourage dogs to run faster), although illegal, still occurs.

CIRCUSES

Highly sensitive, social and intelligent animals such as elephants are held captive in small cages, wagons or enclosures, and are only released to perform tricks for our 'entertainment'. Circuses have been declining in popularity for decades and bans or restrictions on the use of wild animals have been spreading across the world. At the time of writing, 45 countries and 32 US states have introduced such laws. California's Governor signed a bill in 2019 which prohibits 'a person from exhibiting or using any animal other than a domestic dog, domestic cat, or domesticated horse in a circus in this state'.[16] In Australia, there are sadly no national welfare standards for circus animals, let alone a ban. It's up to us to say no to cruel entertainment and send these unethical relics out of business.

RODEOS

Using the old-fashioned rodeo to demonstrate riding and farmed-animal-handling skills is a long-standing tradition in many countries, including Australia, USA, Canada, Mexico, Brazil and Argentina. But despite their glamorous cowboys, parades and prizes, rodeos are occasions rife with fear, pain and stress. Events like calf-roping involve animals being lassoed and jerked by the neck, sometimes resulting in painful injuries, such as punctured lungs, or paralysis, or death. Due to animal-welfare concerns, rodeos have been banned in the UK and Netherlands, with many other nations placing restrictions on certain practices.

Eating Out

We want to support vegan businesses as much as we can, but finding a vegan restaurant or cafe in your area (or convincing your friends to join you at one) can sometimes be hard. It's depressing to look at a menu and find yourself with little to eat, so when you go out with friends or family, be prepared with these easy tips.

LEARN ABOUT DIFFERENT CUISINES

There are many different types of cuisines that can adapt very well to vegan diets and are now accessible in big cities. Stay away from steakhouses and barbecue houses and focus on the many cuisines that can easily convert from vego to vegan.

Some vegans list the most vegan-friendly foods as those coming from the Middle East, Ethiopia and Japan. The reasonably vegan-friendly ones are considered to be Greek, Thai, Chinese and Mexican, with Italian limited and Indian and French challenging. These categories aren't always foolproof, though, and can depend on the region. After spending time in Europe, Issie Saker says, 'Finding food in traditional Greek restaurants has been hard while southern Italy is full of good local vegie dishes. Provence is great for vegan-friendly foods and I once ate my best meal ever there – a vegan ratatouille.' Meg Good often opts for vegan versions of Italian pizzas and pastas and I'm most partial to Thai rice noodles and Japanese eggplant.

CHOOSE THE RESTAURANT

If you're going out with family or friends, ask to choose the restaurant yourself so you can research menus and vegan-friendly restaurants beforehand. They may even be happy to go to a vegan restaurant with you – check out the ones in your area by using an app such as HappyCow. If the restaurant has already been chosen and you know it's not vegan friendly, ask (in your most endearing voice!) if you can change it.

SPEAK TO THE WAITER

Call restaurants before you go so they know you're vegan and have time to prepare. Otherwise, explain your restrictions to the waiter and ask for substitutions or even a special meal. I find that waiters are often helpful, giving me tips on which dishes on the menu the chef can easily adapt or they go to ask the chef directly what's on offer. If the staff are super helpful and cooperative, make sure to compliment them and visit as often as possible. But for those who meet you with disdain, don't give them your repeat dollar.

CHECK FAST FOOD

There's a growing list of fast-food restaurants that now have vegan dishes. It's not good to make a habit of eating fast food – but if you find yourself staring at a list of burgers, you may just get lucky and find a plant-based one. If they don't state something is vegan, you can also check online to make sure that their vegan-looking foods (such as chips) have no hidden animal ingredients.

KEEP POSITIVE

If all else fails, have a snack before you go out and focus on the side dishes and salads. Don't let your vegan diet become such an issue with good friends that you stop wanting to spend time with them. With the right attitude from everyone, a happy compromise can always be found.

Travel

Travelling can be challenging for a newly minted vegan, but worry no more! Here are five tips to help you on your way:

RESEARCH

Make note of vegan-friendly restaurants, health-food stores and markets before you go. There are awesome apps to download. HappyCow finds vegan restaurants and shops close to your location, anywhere in the world where travellers frequent. It's user-driven, so remember to add and rate as you go. Issie says, 'I always research restaurants in the city I'm travelling to and check their reviews online before I go. I make a list of five to six places in the area I'll be staying in and email the place in advance before I confirm the booking to make sure they can cater for me.' Also, research the most popular meals in the country you're travelling to in order to make sure there aren't hidden animal products. For example, some Asian foods, such as agedashi tofu, contain fish sauce in what would seem to be an otherwise vegan meal, while vegan-looking food in India often contains ghee (clarified butter).

TAKE FOOD

Travelling on planes, trains, boats and automobiles can be particularly hard for a vegan. When I'm hangry – hungry and irritable! – finding a decent vegan meal at an airport or train station can make me want to cry. So pretend you're a squirrel, stock up on nuts and store them in your bag. Snacks like dried fruit or even a container of hummus and a bag of crackers can make a huge difference to a trip's success. Remember, of course, to book a vegan meal when you fly. At least you'll have the plane trip covered.

BRING SOME ESSENTIALS

If you're using vegan toiletries, travel with them in small containers (less than 100 millilitres) in your carry-on or put them into your large bag. Bring along your B12 vitamins as well as any other supplements you take. You can also pack some super foods, such as chia or hemp seeds, or protein powder in case you struggle to find healthy vegan options for a few days.

CONNECT WITH LOCALS

Instagram is an awesome platform for vegan food inspiration. Search for the name of the place you're going to, add 'vegan' and you'll find locals and travellers galore who have posted pics of their fave vegan dishes and restaurants. If you're feeling bold, send a local vegan a message asking for advice. Who knows, you may even make a friend!

LEARN A FEW WORDS

In some countries, the word 'vegan' (or even 'vegetarian') isn't readily translated or understood. The term 'meat' may not refer to pork or chicken, for example. Instead, you may have to list each of the products you don't eat. Ask a fluent speaker to write down the key words and either learn how to pronounce them or write them clearly in a handy notebook ready to point to.

GEMMA DAVIS

Gemma is a naturopath, founder of The Compassionate Road, author of *The Compassionate Kitchen* and an ambassador for Voiceless.

WHY I BECAME VEGAN

I gave up meat when I was 18 after working in Hong Kong, where they hang carcasses in the windows of the restaurants. That's when I fully realised the meat I was eating was from a dead animal! A couple of years later, my father started dating his partner, Jenny, who'd been vegan for 20 years. She got me onto Peter Singer's classic, *Animal Liberation*, and I never looked back. I could no longer justify supporting any animal cruelty just for my tastebuds. So, it was firstly for compassionate reasons towards the animals we share this planet with, but I learnt very quickly it was also a choice that matched my values of sustainability and health.

ON FINDING VEGAN FASHION

Google. Really. Thank goodness. I check PETA list or Cruelty-free list when buying products, especially if they are not certified. It is tempting to buy something you like the look of or you heard great things about, but you never know if they still test on animals. I also try buying natural where possible, as I know what we use in our home and on our skin also affects health of everyone. For vegan fashion, I now try to also buy sustainable products from companies that are transparent on what materials they use, their stance on waste and human work conditions.

WHAT I LEARNED ABOUT HEALTH

When I first changed to vegan, I had to unlearn the marketing about needing dairy for calcium. I also realised I couldn't slack off and just eat pasta; I needed a diet of wholefoods. It helped that I was a naturopathic student at the time. Even so, at the start, I thought soy was the answer to everything and depended on it too much. I now wish I'd had someone who could have

showed me simple recipes or food choices that weren't all soy. Luckily, now there are so many choices: of nut milks that taste great, of coconut yoghurts, nut cheeses and lentil burgers.

MY ADVICE FOR STAYING HEALTHY

Keep in mind why you've chosen to be vegan. It isn't generally something people choose without a moral reason – animal-cruelty reasons, sustainability or for their health. Remembering these reasons means we're more likely to make healthy choices so we can stay vegan. If we eat rubbish and get sick, we'll likely blame it on being vegan – not that we ate badly. So, don't forget the why!

And then, eat a wholefood-based diet: more from the earth, less from packages. Make what you eat count, so don't skip meals to have a coffee or eat the cake from morning tea because you'll be missing the opportunity to eat something nutritious that will fill you up with vitamins and minerals.

Limit or avoid the foods and drinks that put you on the back foot – you know the ones ... caffeine, sugar, artificial flavours and colours and alcohol. These bind with nutrients and excrete them from your body or put extra pressure on your body.

Make sure you have a healthy digestive system. If you don't, go see a naturopath for some herbal support to get it functioning well, otherwise it doesn't matter what you eat, you won't absorb the nutrients.

Lastly, stress less. Or have a practice where you can calm and centre yourself to deal with stress. Stress affects every system of the body. We can eat all the organic mung beans in the world, but if we're strung out, we won't stay healthy!

Pets

Can pets go vegan too? Today more and more vegans are seeking vegan food for their pets, causing impressive growth in this new market. But veganism for pets can still be viewed as highly controversial. All animal lovers, vegan or otherwise, want to protect their beloved pets and not risk their health.

Let's focus on our common friends, cats and dogs. As we have long suspected, they are very different both in their characters and in their diet too.

Cats are obligate carnivores, and in the wild their diet can consist of rodents, reptiles, birds and small fish.[17] A cat's nutritional needs are more complex than a dog. Cats require proteins and amino acids, like taurine, that are naturally found in meat. Cats can't synthesise key nutrients from vegetables so vegan cats *must* be given the correct supplements otherwise it's dangerous to their health.

Dogs are omnivores. Unlike cats, they can find most of their nutrients in plants. However, they do need a very carefully designed diet and possibly nutritional supplements if they are forgoing animal products. The nutritional needs of many (not necessarily all) cats and dogs can be met with a mixture of a specialised vegan diet and supplements that can be found in high-quality commercial vegan pet food.

Harry Bolman faced international backlash when news spread that he feeds his cat a vegan diet. In response, Harry said, 'My whole lifestyle is devoted to saving animals and the Earth. I'd never do anything to hurt my pets.' His beautiful feline, Uma, eats a vegan diet supplemented with plant-based alternatives to taurine and arginine (found in commercial vegan cat food), which are usually only found in animal products. He continued: 'I've always refused to have animal products in my house and Uma has been a vegan cat ever since I first adopted her. She absolutely loves her vegan diet. I will boil some pumpkin and mash it up with the dry vegan cat food and she chows it down like there is no tomorrow. Uma is very healthy, she's got the whitest coat, a great appetite and is full of vitality. Regular processed cat food is abysmal. It's just bits and pieces of different animals, which is absolutely revolting.'

Talk to your current vet or find one who has experience with vegan pets. You need someone with sound knowledge and expertise to properly advise you on this journey. A vet may also suggest more frequent check-ups to monitor your pet during the transition.

Some pets can be picky when it comes to changes in their food, but their digestive systems will also need some time to adjust. Start by mixing their regular food with the new food, and then slowly adjust the ratio. If your pet needs encouragement, try enticing them with catnip, olive oil or nutritional yeast.

FINDING A PET

How you come to find your next furry best friend isn't a strictly vegan issue, but, #sorrynotsorry, I think it's super important so I'm including it here! It breaks my heart knowing there are millions of desperate animals looking for forever homes while at the same time puppy mills (the equivalent of factory farms for dogs) are pumping out dogs in the millions. Puppy mills breed all kinds of dogs (from golden retrievers to shih tzu) who are often found for sale through ads in classifieds and in pet stores. The female dogs, or 'breeders', are kept permanently in cages. The female has litter after litter of puppies, all of whom are taken away causing her distress and feelings of isolation. Cages can be stacked up high and the faeces from the dogs in the higher cages fall through to the lower dogs, covering them with urine and excrement. There's usually no veterinary care, and dogs suffer numerous health issues. Once the female can no longer produce pups, she might be shot.

One also has to be very careful with registered breeders, as there is a serious lack of adequate laws or even enforcement to ensure puppies or kittens are treated well and the term 'registered breeder' has no uniform meaning. Backyard breeding operations can also be rife with cruelty. Never buy a puppy or a kitten unless you've seen where they have been raised and are satisfied with the conditions. If the breeder isn't keen to show you their place, you can be certain there are issues.

Often we want a breed because, along with aesthetics, we believe a certain dog comes with a certain character. Pit bull? Dangerous. Golden retriever? Child-friendly. This is often not the case. Look up 'pit bulls and babies' on YouTube and you'll be immersed in a world of sweetness. Individual dogs have their own unique character and personality, so let go of control – animals are not made to order.

Purebred dogs and cats can also have increased incidences of inherited diseases and heightened health issues thanks to generations of selective inbreeding. Brachycephalic breeds of dog ('brachy breeds'), including pugs, french bulldogs and shih tzu, have been bred to have wrinkly faces and bulging eyes, just because we think it's cute. For them, having a raft of problems including breathing difficulties, a higher tendency to collapse in the heat, sleep apnoea, eye disease and difficulty giving birth because of their large heads relative to their bodies is not cute at all.[18] Persian cats, for similar reasons, have high levels of dental and eye problems.

Cavalier king charles spaniels are beautiful dogs but half of them will develop mitral valve disease, which can result in premature death. German shepherds suffer from hip dysplasia, and toy and miniature dog breeds suffer from persistent dislocation of the kneecap. We bought our second dog Taurus when Bronnie was already quite elderly. He was a blue doberman, absolutely gorgeous and as sweet as agave syrup. He was the least dangerous canine on Earth (although many people were terrified of him, especially when he ran to put his head between men's legs as his way of hugging them!) and he died way too young, at just four years old, from a breed-related problem called cardiomyopathy, which is an enlarged heart. Losing Taurus caused heartbreak in our family. The take-home message? It's ideal to adopt an animal from a shelter. The good news is that shelters are found in every area and are full of beautiful dogs and cats.

Fact: **Bramble Heritage** was one of the world's longest living dogs. She was also a vegan. A border collie usually lives to 14 years, but Bramble lived to be 25 and ate a varied diet, including brown rice, lentils, textured vegetable protein, herbs and yeast extract.[19]

Advocacy

For many vegans, changing our lifestyle can still feel like we're not doing enough. We want to do more, make a bigger difference. That's where advocacy comes in. Not only is it immensely satisfying to do something meaningful, with altruistic behaviour often increasing our own happiness, but it can make a huge difference to the lives of others and the health and ultimate survival of our Earth.[20]

Fact: **The world's largest animal rights march in history was in Tel Aviv in 2017 with over 30,000 people taking to the streets to protest against animal cruelty and promote veganism.**

I know from personal experience that getting active can bring great joy and satisfaction. My life, since I first encountered activism as a teenager, became immeasurably enriched by the many meaningful, purpose-drive experiences I engaged in. I tried many a route to express my concern for animals, from public protests, leafleting, to volunteering my time at non-profit organisations. And to this day, despite the challenges and frustrations, I cannot imagine my life without animal advocacy. Spreading your wings into the world of advocacy could also surprise you by not only being good for your soul, but also making a real-life positive impact on animals and our environment. Choose an advocacy style that suits your personality; it will help you last for the long haul. Changing the world is a marathon, not a sprint!

If you're an introvert like me, your style may look quieter than speaking to world leaders at the UN like Greta Thunberg. Activities such as advocacy through writing or researching may be a better fit. But never fear – quieter people can make a difference too. Take it from Mahatma Gandhi, who overturned British control of India using the philosophy of non-violence: 'In a gentle way, you can shake the world.'

If you love being around people or like being in the limelight, you could organise a protest or jump-start a campaign. How about your own vegan YouTube channel or even a vibrant life in politics? Why not?

TIM VASUDEVA

An experienced animal advocate, Tim is now Director of Corporate Affairs at Animals Australia.

WHAT INSPIRED ME TO GO VEGAN

I'd been vegetarian since 2002 but it wasn't until I started working for Animal Welfare League New South Wales and RSPCA South Australia that I began to understand more about the inherent cruelty of industries like dairy, eggs and wool, and the extent to which farm animals are exempt from the animal-cruelty protections provided by legislation. Having overseen about 10,000 cruelty reports and 100 prosecutions each year while at RSPCA South Australia, I know first-hand that it's true that the invasive surgeries routinely and legally performed by farmers on farm animals without anaesthetic would attract jail time if a dog or cat were subjected to the same treatment. Cutting out dairy and eggs and making kinder choices with things like clothing wasn't difficult once I became aware of the suffering those industries impose on so many animals.

THE MOMENT EVERYTHING CHANGED

King was my first ever companion animal. He was a big boofy ginger rescue cat and weighed about 10 kilograms. He wasn't overweight, just a naturally huge cat with an enormous wide fluffy head and massive tail. He had the most amazing personality and would follow me around the house and chat away as if we were having a regular conversation. When he was nine, he just keeled over one evening after eating his dinner. I tried to give him mouth to mouth, but he didn't make it. Our vet thought that perhaps he had a ruptured aneurysm, as he couldn't find any other explanation. He was otherwise very healthy.

For several months after King's passing I was very depressed as it was so unexpected. Eventually, it occurred to me that one of the reasons his death had affected me so much was that I'd gotten

to know him and his personality. And if a cat could have such an amazing personality, why would I assume that other animals wouldn't be similar? Could I really be okay with eating animals who were also full of life and individuals in their own right? Was it okay that I could cause them harm because I just hadn't gotten to know them, given I could never do that to an animal I did know? I decided I'd stop eating meat for a while to see how I felt and whether it made me feel better. After about a month I realised I didn't feel any worse physically, but I did feel a lot better emotionally. Eventually, it felt like my way of honouring King and acknowledging the impact he had on my thinking, which has been my inspiration to continue making those kinder choices.

I didn't take the next step to become vegan for a number of years after that, but King certainly put me on the path of looking at animals as individuals, which would eventually lead me there.

ADVICE FOR NEW VEGANS

Everyone's journey is individual. I know very few people who just went from eating meat to being vegan overnight, so don't expect the rest of the world to do just that. If you've made these important decisions yourself and want others to join you, respect that others will process information and make decisions at their own speed and in accordance with the timeline that works for them. This is particularly important if their decision to move away from animal products is to become a sustained one – they have to make that choice because it means something to them and is therefore sustainable. Badgering, haranguing or abusing people just makes them dig their heels in. You have to be patient and try to bring them with you at their own speed.

The ethical argument about animal suffering isn't always what persuades people. Some people are indifferent to animal welfare but are open to discussions about the health or environmental impacts of meat and animal agriculture. There are many paths for people to get to the same outcome.

MY BEST COOKING TIP

Steal other people's ideas! Vegan food is now so mainstream that it's easy to find all the recipes and nutritional information you will ever need online. The days of people claiming that vegan meals are bland or tasteless are well behind us.

TEN EASY IDEAS

1.

Express your views with opinion pieces and letters to the editor and submit to newspapers and magazines. Make sure your letters are responding to an issue that's currently in the news for a better chance of publication.

2.

Write to your local political representative on topical animal issues you care about, such as ending live exports.

4.

Encourage your teachers to include animal protection education in their lessons (check out Voiceless's resources!) and lobby your school, university and workplace cafeterias to be vegan friendly.

3.

Support political parties doing good work by volunteering your time.

5.

Fundraise for an animal group or sanctuary. Fun-runs, online crowd-funding, raffles or even a vegan bake sale can bring in good money.

FOR GETTING ACTIVE

6.

Use hashtags, sign petitions or even start your own one online. A tip: research your issue and be well informed before you speak out.

7.

Post glowing reviews of vegan businesses – your support will help them become successful!

8.

Write public complaints via social media to companies who are failing animals – social media influences their brand, reputation and bottom dollar, giving them plenty of motivation to pull their socks up.

9.

Go to the streets with peaceful protests, sit-ins and leafleting. As famous author Alice Walker wrote, 'Activism is the rent I pay for living on this planet.'

10.

Shareholder activism is powerful. If you have shares in a publicly traded company, you can use your rights to bring about change to their animal-related policies or practices.

HOW TO BE INTERSECTIONAL

More and more vegans are getting behind the philosophy of intersectionality. Here's a little explainer on what it means, in a vegan context, as it's a new term for many people.

Furthering our vision for a better world means stopping oppression of all kinds. Intersectionality aims to address the root issues, merging social justice movements to fight not only cruelty to animals and environmental destruction but all forms of oppression, prejudice, exploitation and harm – such as racism, sexism, ableism, classism, anti-Semitism, Islamophobia, sizeism, ageism, homophobia, transphobia and the many other discriminations ailing our society. This will inevitably lead to our society placing more value on kindness, justice, fairness, freedom and equality.

One of our A-Team members explains that veganism 'dictates my whole lifestyle: to be kind to animals, the Earth, each other; to follow sustainable practices as much as I can; and to always try to leave a light footprint wherever I tread'.

An example of the opposite of intersectionality? Here's one I can imagine: a vegan event that is advertised using only images of thin, young white women; is full of single-use plastics; has no disability access; pays the hospitality staff sub-standard wages; sources produce from farmers working in exploitative conditions; and has a panel of experts featuring only cisgender white men.

To live the most authentic vegan lifestyle, we don't have to be perfect – after all, that's impossible. We don't want to become so overwhelmed by terrible issues that we can no longer take any action. However, in our fight against the exploitation of animals, we should aspire to be as mindful as possible about our fellow humans too, while also protecting our natural world. Akira Isogawa, a famous Australian fashion designer, told us about his intersectional practices:

> 'In my practice animal protection is one important philosophy, but I also make sure that there is no [other] abuse. Humans can be abused as well, especially in third-world countries. I visit countries like India, because certain products do come from India, and make sure toxic chemicals are not used for dyeing, creating a mess in the environment.' [21]

In the United States, there are multiple examples of how veganism has expanded to connect health, animals and social justice with the fight for racial equality.

Many vegan people of colour see food as political and connected to race and oppression, social justice and access. Writer and producer Aph Ko says, 'The black vegan movement is one of the most diverse, decolonial, complex and creative movements.'[22]

Being an intersectional vegan could look as simple as this – someone who:

- ✿ avoids waste, plastic and packaging;
- ✿ is respectful in conversations and on social media with people they passionately disagree with;
- ✿ ensures inclusivity and accessibility for those with physical disabilities, adding captions to videos for people who are hearing impaired, and allows those who can't afford tickets to also attend events.

THE EXPLOITATION OF WOMEN AND ANIMALS

Our meat-eating culture can be, unfortunately, rife with toxic masculinity. Media representations of masculinity often reinforce this – encouraging men to view both women and animals as objects to be consumed, exploited and dominated. Just as women are 'animalised', or seen as lower or less than, in popular culture, animals can be sexualised and feminised. Of course, this kind of stereotyping helps no one, men included. Carol J. Adams has been at the forefront of exploring this intersection between male stereotypes and the sexualisation of women and animals in advertising. Her online archive has endless real-world examples.[23] One ad features a sexy pig-woman in a bra with the words 'Racks for Racks', and another ad for a restaurant shows two real and buxom women behind a platter of barbecued ribs saying, 'We've got the best racks'. There's a truck with a 'sexy' cartoon chicken winking and offering her 'Buns N' Thighs'. In one ad a burger has been given long legs and high heels and a thought bubble that says, 'Eat me', and recently I photographed a restaurant sign with a chicken, posing seductively. She too was saying 'Eat me!'

Another reason to pause for thought is that the connection between the treatment of women and animals is the exploitation of female bodies. Female animals are arguably the most brutally treated in industrialised animal industries. The hen, for example, spends her life producing eggs for our consumption. In order to maximise the natural rhythms of her female body, she is not allowed any hours of darkness. The female cow is exploited for the milk she produces for her young. Forced into cycles of pregnancy and birth, she is never allowed contact with her offspring. Eggs and milk are the most female products available. They are the intimate products of a female's ability to conceive and nurture life. As Natalie Portman said, 'Only after I became active in women's issues did I realize that my veganism was related to those very issues ... Dairy and eggs don't just come from cows and chickens, they come from female cows and female chickens.'[124]

'I think animal rights or animal welfare are related to human dignity; how we look at ourselves and how we can treat other lives with the same kind of respect.'

Ai Weiwei, contemporary artist and activist and Voiceless Patron

5

YOUR
COMMUNITY

'Whatever it is that sparks your calling
to veganism, find those people. There is
strength in numbers and we need to feel
understood and valued when so many
people still do not understand.'

GEMMA DAVIS

Your psychological wellbeing is as important as your physical wellbeing, and one of the most common traits of a happy vegan is having online or IRL friends and a community to lean on and provide support, skills and knowledge.[1] You can find vegans locally or connect with them in countries across the world.

Animal lawyer Sarah Margo offers reassurance and advice: 'Discovering the extent of institutionalised animal suffering can be hugely distressing. It's so important to seek out support if you feel overwhelmed, and to remember that you are not alone – there are millions of people who think like you and are doing amazing work to better the world ... I joined a local community group for vegans, which frequently held events. I then went to a lot of vegan restaurants, markets, festivals and activism events – there's always a community of animal lovers nearby.'

Start creating a constellation of shining vegan lights in your life by:

- ✿ checking out local vegan-friendly markets, restaurants and stores;
- ✿ going high-tech. There's a plethora of vegan food apps, podcasts and YouTubers;
- ✿ following vegan recipe sites, joining Facebook groups and online forums and subscribing to newsletters;
- ✿ travelling to a vegan festival or animal rights event – they're popping up in cities around the world;
- ✿ finding local groups or places where you can chat with real-life vegans;
- ✿ telling people in advance you're vegan at social gatherings. You may find other vegan friends there too. And a vegan cookbook is a perfect gift!

Posting, tweeting, sharing and commenting in vegan online communities can be immensely helpful and rewarding.In fact, it may be the difference between staying the course or not. Around 84 per cent of former vegetarians and vegans said they were not actively involved in a vegetarian/vegan group or organisation like a potluck or online community.[2] But, please, be careful of the haters and finger-pointers who are unfortunately present in many online vegan groups. Their negativity is unhelpful and can even be harmful. The rate of vegan recidivism is high and caused in part by these attitudes. We need more kindness and less judgement within the vegan community.[3]

There are many organised vegan groups on social media, as well as websites and magazines, giving voice to the growing communities of different ethnicities, sizes, colours, genders, sexualities and disabilities who are moving towards a cruelty-free lifestyle. Examples include those who identify themselves as Plant-Based Māori, Black Vegan, Vegans of Color and LGBTQIA+ Vegan. Take a look and find the hashtag or community most suitable for you – or begin one yourself!

'Whether we're talking about gender inequality or racism or queer rights or indigenous rights or animal rights, we're talking about the fight against injustice. We're talking about the fight against the belief that one nation, one people, one race, one gender or one species has the right to dominate, control and use and exploit another with impunity.'

Joaquin Phoenix

No matter who you are and where you come from, there is sure to be an in-real-life or virtual community waiting to embrace you.

'SOMETIMES, ESPECIALLY IN THE EARLY DAYS, IT CAN BE VERY HARD TO TALK ABOUT ISSUES YOU FEEL SO STRONGLY ABOUT WITH PEOPLE WHO MAY BE CRITICAL OF OR CYNICAL ABOUT YOUR POSITION. YOU HAVE NO OBLIGATION TO DISCUSS YOUR FEELINGS WITH YOUR FRIENDS IF YOU ARE NOT YET READY TO DO SO. JUST LEADING BY EXAMPLE CAN HAVE SIGNIFICANT FLOW-ON EFFECTS IN ITSELF.'

DR MEG GOOD, VOICELESS ANIMAL LAW AND EDUCATION MANAGER

ZOE BORBIRO WITH HER SONS, KYLE, EDAN AND CASPER

Zoe has been vegan since 1991. She's raising a vegan family with three sons: Casper, 6 years; Edan, 17 years; and Kyle, 18 years.

HOW I STARTED MY JOURNEY

Zoe: I became vegetarian at 10 years and vegan when I was 13. I was first inspired to become vegan while reading Peter Singer's *Animal* Chay Neal

A long-time vegan, Chay is Executive Director at Animal Liberation Queensland.
when I was a vegetarian. I was certain that being vegan was ethically essential and inevitable for me. At the same time I was unsure as to how I would survive nutritionally. It took a few years until I heard my conscience definitively confirm 'I am vegan now' and I knew nothing would override that.

MY AH-HA MOMENT

Kyle: I don't recall having one profound experience which solidified my confidence that veganism was right for me.

Rather, it's the cumulative comfort of knowing that, to the small amount practicable, I'm not contributing to animal suffering.

Edan: While there was no single experience that convinced me to stay vegan, every experience I have with animals, whether it be with dogs at home or animals in a sanctuary, furthers my stance on animal rights.

Zoe: I was on holiday with my family and during a walk saw a fish suffering on a pier. The fish was writhing in pain and I asked my dad why the person who caught it wasn't putting the fish in a bucket of water or killing it. His response was, 'It doesn't matter. They're going to eat it anyway.' As a child I'd been fishing several times and had always been distracted by my own enjoyment of the surrounding nature and company. But in that moment, all I could see and feel was the fish's pain. I knew

I never wanted to be part of such suffering so I never ate sea animals again and after a few months stopped eating the flesh of others completely.

ADVICE FOR NEW VEGAN FAMILIES

Zoe: The moments that can seem incredibly confronting will often lead to the best outcomes for your vegan family and those around you. Work through social discomfort and always align your actions with your ethics, even if it's challenging in the moment.

FAVOURITE FOODS

Zoe: Eating out – fried everything. At home – bowls of rice, tofu, nuts and vegetables. Sushi.

Kyle: Corn chips and salsa; homemade tacos; and baguettes with hummus.

Edan: Taco, taquito and souvlaki.

Casper: Sushi. Lord of the Fries.

COOKING

Zoe: Keep it simple. I learned a long time ago not to spend more than 15 minutes preparing a meal.

MY IDEAL WORLD

Kyle: An ideal world would be vegan. However, I am cognisant of the fact that this is a long way off. In the shorter term, I believe that 'clean' meats and other vegan meats could potentially play a large role in the widespread adoption of veganism.

Edan: I believe that an ideal world – and the direction that the world is moving in, slowly but surely – would be all vegan. The problems that the world is facing with climate change and the many leading diseases causing death could be solved or aided if everyone was vegan.

Zoe: An ideal world would be vegan. Intersectional veganism is key in alleviating oppression.

Family and friends

Suddenly, we are aware of a terrible injustice happening around us, an awful, horrible, unacceptable situation. We've seen pictures and videos, read the information, and the veil has been lifted; our eyes are wide open to the horrors that animals are subjected to, from exploitation and cruelty to suffering and violence. Climate change and the destruction of the environment are also top of our minds.

And yet, our closest family and friends don't always follow our lead or join us on this journey or, worse, they roll their eyes or make unfunny jokes or dismissive comments. This can be extremely upsetting for new vegans who are feeling full of passion and emotion and are often especially sensitive souls.

Sometimes we find that our beloved circle fail to:

- look or listen to what we are showing or telling them;
- believe us that this is real, that this is really happening;
- care about the subject at all; and/or
- respect our point of view, which feels like a lack of respect for us.

We can't help but wonder – how can they not see, feel, believe, act? There are powerful forces at work that are preventing them from doing so. Some of us have managed to break out of the Matrix and reach the other side. Others have not, cannot and will not. All for different reasons. We can explain, argue, cajole, plead, cry and shout. And it will lead to nothing except fractured relationships and our own sense of isolation, bitterness and resentment.

Clare Mann, a vegan psychologist, calls this 'vystopia', a suffering unique to vegans who struggle to live in a non-vegan world with people who don't seem to care. She found that 59 per cent of vegans were the only vegan in their family and 51 per cent had a disinterested partner.[4] When people we love don't change, we feel like they are colluding with systemised cruelty while we're traumatised and even ridiculed or criticised. We can't allow this to cause disillusion or cut us off from our friends and family. That is not good for us, and not good for the animals we are aiming to protect either.

VEGAPHOBIA

Many, many vegans report that their transition was easy-as-vegan-pie. But there can be challenges to overcome. Be aware that your decision to go vegan can raise the hackles of your friends and family; they might take your decision as a judgement of *their* values or choices. And even though it's not about *them*, it's about *you* – how you feel, the life you want to lead, the compassion in your heart, and your desire for a just, fair, non-violent world – they sometimes don't get it.

This defensive reaction is so widespread it has been studied by researchers and aptly titled 'vegaphobia'.[5] But don't despair, it's just their pre-conditioned ideas and natural defence mechanisms kicking in. Here are a few thoughts on why some people may have a negative reaction to your vegan journey.

- ❀ **It requires change.** If other people agreed with us off the bat, acknowledged that going vegan is a win–win, then logic would dictate that they too would have to make the change. That requires their energy to change their diet and habits. Nobody wants to work hard if they don't have to. Instead, they try to poke holes in our 'argument', to save themselves a lot of time and effort.
- ❀ **Veganism gets a bad rap.** Veganism is often discredited and ridiculed in the media and vegans stereotyped as angry, militant, self-denying, sentimental, faddy or joyless. One study reports that

vegans are associated with being fussy, awkward, wealthy, hippie, extreme, radical, overly healthy, under-nourished and even too feminine. This brings me to the next point.

❀ **It challenges male stereotypes.** Being vegan is seen as girly because meat is often inherently linked to manhood and closely implicated in the construction of masculine identity. Men who don't eat meat are, therefore, often portrayed as weak and effeminate.

❀ **It questions our identity.** What we eat marks our social and cultural identity and, in our western culture, eating meat is seen as normal and natural.[6] If someone criticises our diet, even if it's only implied, it can threaten the identity we depend on and feel hurtful, like a personal slight.

❀ **It can seem holier-than-thou.** Vegans can be seen as preachy, which can cause anger. Research has shown that vegans can cause defensiveness among non-vegans by implying a moral failure. In one study, 47 per cent of participants freely associated negative terms with vegetarians because they expected vegetarians to see themselves as morally superior.[7]

TALKING TO YOUR NON-VEGAN LOVED ONES

Maintaining good relationships may be the greatest challenge on our vegan journey. Here is some hard-won advice for how to successfully engage in a conversation about your choice to go vegan. You may also decide to opt out of a conversation that seems fruitless and frustrating. We want to walk that fine line between being open for conversation and looking after ourselves.

Research and prepare

Often our family and friends have our best interests at heart and the first thing they need reassurance about is nutrition. Do your research and explain clearly how you plan to become a healthy, strong, thriving vegan. Once you've ticked off that box, you can, if you want to, broach the issues that led you to go vegan.

Gemma suggests providing cold, hard facts: 'Ones that are non-debatable, that come from research from the UN or are government statistics. Whether they be about global warming impact, or health issues, or why I don't wear leather ... I always keep it short but direct. I never tell them they are doing something wrong, but back up why it is that I make choices.'

About talking to parents, Avalon Llewellyn, author of *The Modern Day Guide to Going Vegan at a Young Age*, recommends, 'First do your research on nutrition, ethics, religion and anything you think your parents will want to know about. It can take a lot of guts to talk to your parents, especially if they are averse to change.'

Lead by example

Focus on why you are choosing to start this journey. This helps get people open to listening, to hearing. It's harder to argue against someone's personal decision, rather than a philosophical or moral position, especially if it's not hurting anyone else. After I became vegetarian, it took my family between 5 and 25 years to follow suit. Some friends stopped eating pork, others all meat, and a few surprised me years later with their decisions to fully change their diets.

Shaun Moss, from the A-Team, says, 'I'm honest when I say that becoming vegan is the best thing I have ever done, and this gets people interested.' Melissa Hobbs advises, 'If you make people "wrong", it puts them in a position where they feel the need to defend. I prefer to ask questions and talk about why I've made the decisions I have.'

Be patient and stay strong

It can take time for our loved ones to adjust. Bailey Mason, a young vegan activist, advises, 'I know it can be a kick in the guts to feel that even your friends don't support your veganism ... Be patient with your friends and family as they get to understand your lifestyle.' Some people, despite your patience and explanations, will not understand. And that's okay. Corelle Gabay, a teenage vegetarian (and my niece), says, 'Your friends should understand your decision and, even if they don't like it, it's your own decision. Just ignore their bad attitude if you need to.'

Identify allies

Often friends and family will show support for your veganism in subtle ways. We might get angry that they're not adapting their own diet, but perhaps they go out and buy you a vegan cake when you visit, or note a new cruelty-free shop that's opened nearby. A friend of mine always researches local vegan restaurants whenever I'm in town and, even though I don't ask her to do it, she never orders meat in front of me. People like this are on their way to becoming your vegan *allies*.

Dr Melanie Joy, psychologist and author of *Beyond Beliefs: A Guide to Improving Relationships and Communication for Vegans, Vegetarians and Meat Eaters*, explains: 'An ally stands beside you even if your paths are different. An ally has your back even if your cause is not the same. An ally may not share your views, but they fully understand and respect those views and they fully support and respect you for who you are and what you believe.[18]

And as much as you might want them to also start on a vegan journey themselves, being an ally is still an important role. Allies can be a support network, even if their beliefs or behaviours differ to yours. Give them positive reinforcement for their acts of support and be thankful and grateful for what they do rather than focusing on what they don't do.

Show kindness

Remain positive and understanding of people's position as well as mindful of your own emotional state. A-Team member Dr Meg Good says, 'Unfortunately some people will feel confronted by your decision to go vego. They may challenge you, ask intrusive questions and just generally attempt to undermine your decision.'

This is a great opportunity to learn how to speak to others who have differing views. As Meg says, 'Always remain positive and understanding as you were probably once in their position, and you may be the only person in their life presenting them with your perspective.'

Gemma Davis adds, 'I make sure I am tuned into not being judgemental or righteous in any way – that instead I am grounded and coming from a place of love.'

Katrina Fox, journalist and author, agrees: 'Don't make it about you as the self-righteous person versus the other person. Use inclusive, kind language. Be friendly and open to invite curiosity from the other person.'

Woo them with yummy food

Be generous with your friends and family – bring vegan dishes to their homes and gift them inspiring cookbooks. Tamzen Armer from the A-Team describes herself as a 'baketivist' merging baking and activism. Love it! She says, 'If I feed people great vegan options, they see that it's not hard to be vegan.

Most, I think, understand the why, but don't know how.' Diddy Mymin, also from our A-Team, says, 'I love cooking food or baking cakes that non-vegans really enjoy, and then pointing out that it is vegan.'

Tailor your answers

If someone genuinely asks why you are going vegan, tailor your answer to them. Not everyone is interested in animals – perhaps a discussion about climate change or the environment may be the right approach.

Demonstrate compassion

Practise empathy and compassion even in the face of the most frustrating interactions. Humans deserve it as much as animals do. Most of us have been raised with the belief that eating, wearing and using animals is normal, natural and necessary. We were all once there – blind to the consequences of our diets and lifestyles.

We are certainly complex creatures, us humans, and even if we believe something to be correct, we aren't always able to act. Sometimes people have hidden concerns or issues that we are not privy to, such as a fear of hunger caused by a past personal or family trauma or even a highly emotional relationship with food firmly rooted in childhood. For example – *If I stop eating chicken soup, I would betray my beloved grandmother's memory and legacy.* Or – *Putting steaks on the barbecue is something I have always done with my dad, it's how we bond.*

Perhaps this person will, one day, feel strong enough to adapt the soup to vegan and start a new family tradition or find a new way to bond with their father. You don't know. Maybe they're having a supremely hard time at the moment, dealing with disease, disability, depression or divorce and adding another to-do to their list, however valid, is just unimaginable.

Even though I wanted to go fully vegan for years, I went through a long period of personal challenges when my twin boys were born with severe disabilities. We sent doctor to doctor searching for a diagnosis and needed (and still do) a huge amount of early intervention therapies. I just didn't have the mental or emotional energy to make the change. When I re-found some kind of balance in my life, I made veganism my priority. If someone had guilt-tripped me at that difficult time in my life, it would have achieved nothing except a souring of our relationship along with shame and resentment.

We can't know everything that goes into a person's decision-making. And often they don't either. There are subconscious forces at work. Have compassion for people's shortcomings and perceived failures, including your own.

Vegan strategist Tobias Leenaert suggests always taking into account where people are coming from, what time they are living in, and what the norms of the day are before we judge and condemn. If we do that, we will see quite easily why not everyone is doing what we are doing.

Avalon Llewellyn cautions us to approach people with kindness because 'once you were in the same place as them'.

Think strategically

Sometimes one's unspoken or assumed role in the family – the overly sensitive son, rebellious sister or dramatic uncle – can prevent other family members from really listening to that person's message. Rather, they might be more open to hearing it from someone else. Perhaps they have a deep trust in medical doctors or naturopaths, or are avid readers or passionate documentary watchers. Instead of repetitively telling them what you know and believe to no avail, use a variety of other tools. Set up a conversation between them and someone they're already in the habit of listening to, buy them a book, ask them to join you at a local vegan festival for a coconut frappe or suggest a good doco on Netflix. (Start with the resource suggestions at the end of this book.) But remember, don't pressure them or ask if they've seen or read it every time you see them!

Let go and accept

Some people will never move towards a vegan life. Yes, it might be very hard for us to accept, especially if it's a loved one like a partner, parent or child, but it's possible to come to terms with it. Pay attention to the attributes they do have – perhaps they volunteer for the homeless, donate what they can to charity, or are just all-round kind people in other ways.

Just as I'm not – and you're not – perfect in every sphere, neither are others. Sometimes I throw a glass bottle into a non-recycling bin when I'm out and about because I don't want to carry it home. Or I drive instead of walking a short distance, because, hello laziness. Or I take a longer shower than I should because it just feels good. I can go on!

Nobody practises all the values they preach all the time. Find a way to be okay with that.

SAVING YOUR ENERGY – TWO PEOPLE, TWO APPROACHES

When you go vegan, you have to battle against these negative stereotypes, cultural norms and reactions and seemingly become the spokesperson for all things *plant*.

This doesn't always come easily, especially for those of us who are on the shy or introverted side of the spectrum. My teenage vegetarian daughter, Jasmine, was recently asked this silly hypothetical question, 'If you were on an island and there was only a pig, a knife and a fire ... what would you do?'

New vegans can be thrown into the spotlight, expected to answer every complex question and be the expert on nutrition, evolution, science, philosophy and psychology.

I became vego at age seven and have countered most arguments people throw our way. I've also checked in with our Vegan A-Team about the most frustrating comments they've received and how to best react. Try dividing the people you talk to into two groups: people who truly want to understand your point of view and people who just want an argument. This skill improves with experience.

People truly interested in understanding your point of view

These people will have honest questions, so engage them in a conversation – it's worth it. Without us choosing to be, we are now vegan ambassadors, and sharing our thoughts, knowledge and feelings is helpful. Be a role model, have patience and forgive people for their misconceptions, ignorance or naivety.

Vanessa Jaffe, from our A-Team, doesn't use graphic descriptions of slaughterhouses and cruelty in conversations about her veganism 'unless forced to because someone has pissed me off'. She continues: 'I explain the benefits and I honestly do get very excited about the food that I eat – so I usually give people recipes to try or invite them over for a vegan meal.'

Avalon Llewellyn believes that down-to-earth conversations are vitally important: 'I love having conversations with open-minded people and helping them understand why I am vegan. But if they are just angry and wanting to provoke a response then I just stay calm and keep my answers short.' Another A-team member agrees that we should 'keep our conversations short and sweet if we know they don't really care'.

Which brings us to group two.

People only looking for an argument

Engaging with these people is a waste of your time and energy. Don't get stuck in a conversation with someone whose sole aim is to try to make you look ridiculous or rile you up. Answer quickly and change the topic or move away. We need to look after ourselves too, and becoming emotionally drained every time we socialise is not ideal for our long-term health.

In this regard, Avalon advises new vegans not to waste energy on arguing. She also encourages us not to be disheartened: 'It can be hard to feel good when those you love around you don't agree with what you're doing. Breathe. Walk away. People are often resistant to change, and it may take them a while to get used to the idea.' Similarly, Shira, on the A-Team, cautions us to 'be nice, don't preach, and if they don't get it, just let it go.' A-Team member Miriam Cumming advises, 'When interacting online, block or mute anyone who makes you feel down on yourself. Life is too short for drama.'

Even without discussing our whys and how of veganism, we can make an impression on people just be being ourselves. As author Annie Lamott says, 'Lighthouses don't go running all over an island looking for boats to save, they just stand there shining.'

TEN FRUSTRATING THINGS PEOPLE MAY SAY

People can say some interesting things when we mention we are becoming a vegan! One Instagram advocate, Lucie Johnson from @uglyvegan, even made a tote bag printed with the 'out there' questions and responses vegans regularly receive.

But plants have feelings.

Avocados aren't vegan because of bees.

But tofu is weird.

Where do you get your protein?

Is it not expensive eating so many vegetables?

What if you were stranded on one of those hypothetical desert islands that we're all constantly stuck on?

Our fangs were built to rip and ravage flesh.

How do you dine in restaurants?

But who on earth do you eat?

Are you vegan because it's trendy?

If a pig licked your sandwich would you eat it?

Do you miss cheese?

But lions eat meat so we should too.

Would you drink my breast milk?

I bet you have to eat a lot of salad.

Won't cows go extinct if you stop eating burgers all the time?

I bet you do a lot of yoga.

Buuut baaacon.

How do you get your vitamins?

Does your life suck?

The circle of life.

But I can still call you honey, right?

If you were stuck on a boat in the middle of the ocean would you punch a fish and eat it?

Are your poops normal?

Would you eat a human if they asked you to?

Are you always tired because you don't eat blood?

What makes these questions and comments funny is that Lucie didn't make any of them up: they're all true. I've cut these typical responses back to the top ten questions most vegans are faced with at some time or another, and provided suggested answers.

Top ten questions

1. It's not healthy. Where will you get your iron, protein, calcium, vitamin A, B, C ... [cue 'The Alphabet Song']? You're going to get malnutrition.

2. How do you know that vegies [it always tends to be carrots] don't feel pain too? Can you prove it?

3. Humans have eaten meat since the beginning of time. We're part of the food chain. Are you also going to get lions to stop eating gazelles and make them go vegan too?

4. Look! – the person bares their teeth and taps on their pointy canines – we're carnivores. And not only that, it's part of our evolution and how we got such big brains.

5. If we stopped eating animals, what would happen to all the animals that are alive today? There'd be too many and not enough space for them. By not killing and eating them, you're actually being meaner to animals.

6. If we didn't eat animals, we wouldn't breed animals, and then they wouldn't exist at all. We'd have no more pigs or cows or chickens. You're depriving animals of life.

7.	Being vegan is actually worse for animals. Have you considered all the ants and bugs killed when we grow crops? Way more than the other animals.

8.	My aunt/cousin/friend once tried going vegan. And she/he/they got sick with fatigue/ulcers/rash [insert any sickness]. It's very dangerous.

9.	What a #firstworldproblem. What about starving children? Do you want them to stop eating the meagre food they have as well? You should feel grateful to have what you have at all. You are being spoilt, privileged, ungrateful ... [and so on].

10.	If you were stranded in a forest, on a desert island [or in another solely carnivorous galaxy], would you eat meat then?

And two more for good luck:

11.	Why do you care about animals when there are so many other problems in the world – poverty, war, slavery, racism, sexism, inequality ... Animals should be the least of our worries.

12.	It's free-range, grass-fed, cage-free, so it's okay!

If you have experienced any of the above, or are getting shivers at the thought, don't worry, these reactions are just natural defence mechanisms at work. With the help of the A-Team, I've noted down some possible answers.

First though, always answer calmly and with respect. Getting into heated arguments is rarely a recipe for success. In a calm conversation, often something you say will stick with someone, tickle their brain, and if they hear or read it enough times from enough people, they will make the change too. And you may never even know that you contributed to that change.

I must have had a gazillion conversations with people over the past 30 plus years, with questions and comments ranging from naive to curious to outright obnoxious. Occasionally someone will come up to me at a party and say, 'Do you know that what you said all those years ago about [insert something I don't remember saying] really stuck with me? Today I'm also vego/vegan.' That makes me happy.

Top ten answers

1. A vegan diet can be very healthy. I have researched this subject and know I can get everything I need from a balanced diet of grains, legumes and vegies. The only supplement required is B12; other than that, it's all good. If you like, I can send you some info on plant-based nutrition. Did you know that some of the top athletes in the world are vegan?

2. Carrots are not sentient, and that's science talking, not me. Have you heard of the Cambridge Declaration of Consciousness? It states that the top scientists in the world agree animals have

experience and awareness just like us and most people recognise this fact now. Vegetables cannot and do not suffer like animals. What is driving me to be vegan is my desire to play no part in the suffering of animals. If I can live a healthy, happy life without causing pain to animals, I want to live that way.

3. Most people, me included, are no longer living as hunter gatherers. I'm not going to interfere with a lion's diet, they gotta do what they gotta do. I just know that I can have a healthy diet by being vegan and also live according to my values, and so that's what I'm doing.

4. The shape of our teeth does *point* to the fact (pun intended) that we are naturally omnivorous. But the truth of the matter is, with access to a wide range of food and produce, we can now live healthy lives without eating animal products. Our big brains are allowing us to evolve into kinder *Homo sapiens*. Isn't that amazing?

5. If we didn't eat animals, we would stop breeding animals, that's true. This would be a slow process of decreasing the billions of animals we grow and slaughter every year. If, by some Disneyesque magic spell, the entire world stopped eating animals overnight, the animals who are currently alive today would just live out the span of their natural lives.

6. If we stopped breeding animals for food, it is likely that the current breeds of pigs, cows and chickens (who are genetically selected for rapid

growth and maximum yield of milk, eggs and meat) would slowly disappear. But is it better to not exist than to live your entire life in misery, pain and suffering? If I was a farmed animal, I'd make that choice.

7. When people talk about animals killed while farming vegetables, most are estimates of insects. And while I care about insects too (although, um, mosquitos?), many vegans follow a utilitarian approach, with their main focus on reducing the suffering of the greatest number of *sentient* animals – those we currently know suffer from pain and distress. Sadly, farmers can also accidentally kill wild birds and mammals with tractors, plows and pesticides and also on purpose in order to protect their crops so let's also encourage the growing movement of organic, wildlife-friendly and predator-friendly farming.

8. I'm so sorry to hear about your aunt/cousin/friend. I hope they're okay now. It *can* sometimes be tricky to make sure we are getting a balanced vegan diet, as it can be with any diet. Our Western diet is full of temptations – excess sugar, trans fats, additives, and high salt causing worldwide epidemics of obesity, heart disease and type 2 diabetes. We all need to watch out. That's why I'm making sure to inform myself about nutrition. Please don't worry about me!

9. I'm also concerned about children living in poverty. There's lots of research showing how a vegan diet can actually help address food inequality. Would you like me to send you the UN report explaining

how a global shift towards a vegan diet is vital to save the world from hunger, poverty and the worst impacts of climate change? But ultimately, this is a decision I'm making for myself, because I believe it's the kindest way that I can live.

10. If I were stranded on a desert island and starving, I may even eat another human to survive. Have you seen that film about the plane crash where they all become cannibals? Crazy, right?!

And the answers to the bonus two questions:

11. This is called 'whataboutism' – a popular technique to try to undermine an argument. For example: What about refugees? Or domestic violence? Caring about animals does not mean we don't care about other issues like the horrific amount of violence, poverty and human suffering in the world. It's not a zero-sum game. Quite the opposite: compassion breeds compassion. As the founder of the animal rights movement Professor Peter Singer says, 'Animal Liberation is Human Liberation too.' A recent study confirms this, proving correlation between people who care about animal rights and people who care about the rights of LGBTQIA+ individuals, racial and ethnic minorities, unauthorised immigrants and people on low incomes.[9] And, did you know that some of the greatest animal advocates in history have been instrumental in other social justice

movements? Examples include Frances Power Cobbe, a women's rights activist and suffragette who started the first anti-vivisection organisation in 1875, and Henry Spira, a civil rights activist and one of the most effective animal activists of the 1970s and 1980s. Former High Court judge, The Hon. Michael Kirby is a great example of someone who has dedicated his life to opposing all forms of oppression. He has been at the forefront of some of the great social and legal movements in Australia, such as Aboriginal rights, gay liberation, disability rights and women's rights and is now a vocal proponent of animal protection.

Dr Ash Nayate, a vegan neuropsychologist, explains, 'When we care about one social justice movement, we start caring about them all. Our empathy skills are like muscles; they get strengthened with use. So whether it's sexism, racism, homophobia, or transphobia that we're fighting ... our brain is getting primed to care about all forms of oppression.'[10]

12. Although smaller scale farms may be able to implement 'higher welfare' practices, some cruel practices are inherent to modern animal-use farming in breeding, transporting and slaughtering. This means there are still numerous animal-welfare issues with free-range and 'humane' farming.

Fact: **The largest canine teeth of any land animal are found not in a carnivore but in the herbivorous hippopotamus.**

AVALON LLEWELLYN

Avalon is the author of e-book *The Modern Guide to Going Vegan at a Young Age*. She has been vegan since she was 13.

YOUNG VEGANS TELLING THEIR FAMILIES

Be prepared! It's so important to know what you're going to say to your family and how. If you come well prepared, you're far better off. Make sure to do your research on nutrition, ethics, religion etc. – anything that you think your parents will want to know about. It can take a lot of guts to talk to your parents, especially if they're averse to change. Make sure you choose a good moment to talk to them.

HANDLING NON-VEGAN GET-TOGETHERS

To be honest, I was super nervous at first. I felt pretty uncomfortable and I didn't like bringing it up so I tended to bring my own food and keep quiet about my veganism. As I got a bit more comfortable, I'd let the hosts know beforehand – but would still bring my own food. I'm not a fan of bringing up veganism in social situations as the conversations usually turn sour and messy, so I just steer clear and offer people the chance to try my food if they wish. If it's a big dinner or event, I always bring a dish that can be shared with everyone! I'm a huge fan of baking cupcakes and cookies for everyone.

FAVOURITE THINGS ABOUT BEING VEGAN

Changing the world – I don't really have the words for that feeling. The connection with animals. The community. Veganism has opened up an incredible world for me of intersectional activists willing to teach me so many things. I am forever indebted to some of the first few people I met, who taught me about not only veganism, but activism, human and women's rights, LGBTQIA+ rights, etc.

FINDING VEGAN FRIENDS

The way I first connected was through Instagram. I had an account for animal rights where I used to connect with vegans and also record my thoughts; it documented my transition from meat-eater to vegan. It was so helpful to have information and people on hand to ask for advice. If you follow the influential vegans on Instagram, they often have meet-ups, too. I also used Facebook to join my city's local vegan page.

— Advice for teenagers —

We all want our parents to respect and support us. If you're a teen living at home, it's especially important to get support. Here are some tips on how to talk about your vegan choice with your parents or carers.

EXPLAIN YOUR 'WHY'

Before you speak with people in your inner circle, take a moment to consider the three key reasons a vegan lifestyle is important to you. Focus on explaining, not justifying. Let them know how much thought you've given this change and reinforce that this is your own personal decision that you will follow through in a mature, sensible and healthy way.

Young vegan Bailey Mason advises, 'It's hard with the many emotions but it's important to be calm and collected to tell your family the reasons behind it all. You should be patient with your family as they have been told since they were born that eating animals is normal and necessary.'

KNOW YOUR NUTRITION FACTS

Unhealthy. Extreme. Dangerous. There are so many misconceptions about the vegan diet. We are brought up on a diet of meat, fish, eggs and dairy; it's a cultural norm for many of us and considered an essential part of our meals. So be prepared to address the issue of health and nutrition by arming yourself with information and resources.

'How will you get enough iron?' your mum asks, frowning with concern.

'Excellent question!' you say, handing her a trusted list of vegan iron sources (and sources of the other nutritional must-haves like protein and calcium).

By understanding the changes you need to make to ensure your diet is healthy, you can reassure your parents you'll be eating well. Avalon says, 'As I was a competitive swimmer my mum made me do a blood test and meet with a nutritionist just to settle any worries that my parents had. Once it was approved from the nutritionist it was full steam ahead!'

RESPECT THEIR POSITION

Being the only vegan in a family can be challenging. But don't force your views or lay guilt on your mum, dad, brother or grandma (or the family dog).

Having said that, guilt can sometimes work! Greta Thunberg, teen environmental activist and nominee for the Nobel Peace Prize, started learning about the effects of meat on the environment and animals and then talked to her parents: 'The more I read about this, the more I realized we don't have this under control, so then I started to become worried, and I talked to my parents about it. I kept showing them articles and graphs ... and they were like everyone else ... they always had excuses ... But then I made them feel so guilty ... I kept telling them that they were stealing our future and they cannot stand up for human rights while living that lifestyle, so then they decided to make those changes. My dad is vegan, my mom, she tries – she's 90 per cent vegan.'[11]

Remember my niece, the lovely Corelle Gabay? She describes what happened after she told her parents she wanted to be vegetarian: 'Mum didn't believe it. It was a shock because I loved meat, I was the meat-eater of the family, but my family didn't react as dramatically as I thought they would.'

This doesn't mean you shouldn't try to educate those around you about the plight of animals, the impact of animal agriculture on the climate crisis or how beef cattle ranching is destroying the Amazon. But, if you want people to respect your beliefs, you need to practise the same in return, even if their attitudes make you angry or sad.

EMBRACE SELF-RELIANCE

Be confident in your choice, resolute in your justifications and a role model of a healthy vegan life. Hopefully, your loved ones will be on board with your vegan lifestyle. But they may be sceptical or adversarial; either way, it will take time to adjust the workings of your home. Who cooks the meals in your family? Expecting your parents to cook two separate meals isn't really fair or realistic. Seize the opportunity to create your own meals; you might even inspire your family to eat more vegan meals when you show them how tasty vegan food can be. Learning to cook delicious plant-based meals is a great skill to have, because being vegan is a lifestyle, not a fad, and you've got many meals ahead of you!

HOW TO TALK TO FRIENDS

Telling friends that you're going vegan can cause a mixed bag of reactions. Some may just need time. Corelle talks about her experience at school: 'At first my friends were joking and trying to feed me meat. But it didn't feel like joking. Eventually, after a few weeks, they became supportive. Every day for lunch instead of coming to school with meat, I came with vegetarian foods.' My daughter, Jasmine, a vego from birth, advises other young people, 'Don't try to convince friends to become vego – accept that you won't persuade them.'

Kyle Borbiro, 18, says: 'My non-vegan friends (that is, the majority of my friends) are rather unbiased either way towards my being vegan. During any marginally negative experiences I seize the opportunity to discuss veganism in an open and nonjudgmental manner. However, the vast majority of experiences I have with my peers relating to veganism are genuinely inquisitive, expressing interest in being vegan themselves.' Kyle's brother Edan, who's 17, also has a majority of non-vegan friends. 'They will make the occasional joke or jab my vegan views. Though this is usually in a friendly way, when I bring up a serious point to do with veganism, they will usually listen and stop making jokes.'

Avalon found that the issue wasn't her friends: 'I was surprised at how concerned my friends' parents were. My friends were excited about me going vegan but the random unsolicited advice from their parents when I was at their houses was very bizarre.'

At the end of the day, what we put in our bodies is our own personal choice. If veganism feels like the right decision for you, hopefully your family and friends will be supportive. But, even if they are critical, respect their current position, avoid arguments, and venture forth on this wonderful journey in a considered and healthy way. Learn about your nutritional needs and get inspired by accessing some of the many excellent vegan resources available to you, such as recipe books, apps, vegan blogs, podcasts, documentaries and even video essays. Learn how to prepare your own good food, and build a community (online or in real life) of other vegans to share the journey. You may just find that some of your friends and family will surprise you by joining in.

Fact: **Empathy is wired into our brains through special cells called mirror neurons. They allow us to understand what someone else is going through, like we're having the experience ourselves. Studies suggest that some animals, like chimps, dogs, mice and chickens, also have the capacity for empathy.**[12]

6

THE FUTURE

'We are on the cusp of the deepest,
fastest, most consequential disruption in
food and agricultural production since
the first domestication of plants and
animals ten thousand years ago.'[1]

RETHINKX REPORT

By 2050 the world population is predicted to reach nearly ten billion and, to feed that population, it's widely agreed we must change both the way we farm and the foods we eat.

Minimising animal products is considered essential, with beef consumption in countries like Australia needing to fall by 90 per cent and be replaced by five times more beans and pulses. If we can't meet these targets we risk living beyond the planetary boundaries that define a safe operating space for humanity.[2] Yikes!

What's the answer for our future food? Well, there's some debate, as you can imagine. Futurists (yes, that's a thing) predict we will soon be eating via stick-on patches and pills and drips, as well as drinking jellyfish and algae milk and eating insect bread. They also foresee lab-grown meat, which is expected to be delivered by drones.

But seriously, some experts predict that in ten years the beef and dairy industries will collapse due to new technologies. A report by US-based think-tank RethinkX states, 'The cost of proteins will be five times cheaper by 2030 and ten times cheaper by 2035 than existing animal proteins, before ultimately approaching the cost of sugar.'[13] The report also concludes that plant-based and cell-based 'meats' will be 'more nutritious, healthier, better tasting, and more convenient, with almost unimaginable variety as well as 100 times more land efficient, 10–25 times more feedstock efficient, and 10 times more water-efficient as well as producing less waste'.

Entrepreneur Richard Branson says that in 30 years or so, 'We will no longer need to kill any animals and all meat will either be clean or plant-based, taste the same, and also be much healthier for everyone. One day we will look back and think how archaic our grandparents were in killing animals for food.'[14]

The predictions come from two areas with enormous potential for saving animals and the Earth: plant-based food technology and actual meat grown in labs from animal cells, which is known as 'clean meat'.

Plant-based foods

We don't need to be experts to see how plant-based food is slowly but surely taking over the world. In the United States, nearly half of all adults are consuming plant-based meat or milk, and a billion US dollars has been invested in vegan products, including by companies that dominate the conventional meat market. Plant-based meat alternatives have grown 11% in the US and now bring in $4.5 billion dollars in supermarkets annually. In the last 15 years I've gone from taking my own little carton of soy milk travelling with me (so *not* convenient!) to expecting it to be available everywhere I go and rarely being disappointed.

Multinational food franchises such as KFC, Carls Jr, Burger King, Del Taco, Chipotle, Dunkin' Donuts and McDonald's are now launching plant-based 'meats' to their customers around the globe in the form of burgers, sausages, nuggets and sliders. Sales are growing and are estimated to be worth US$3.7 billion. Egg replacements that mirror taste and texture are now becoming all the rage. The third largest meat producer in the world, Cargill, has stated that finding new forms of cell-based and alternative protein production will be crucial to feeding the Earth's growing human population.

Billionaires such as Bill Gates and Richard Branson have thrown their money behind plant-based food technology, and scores of high-profile business leaders, and even entertainment figures, athletes and musicians, are following their lead. Film directors James Cameron and Sir Peter Jackson have joined forces to create a plant-based food business, and the investors in three-billion-dollar vegan food company Impossible Foods include Serena Williams, Jay-Z, *The Daily Show* host Trevor Noah, Reddit co-founder Alexis Ohanian, Katy Perry, Ruby Rose, Jaden Smith, will.i.am and Grammy award-winning record producer Zedd.

Companies are competing for market share of this burgeoning area with new businesses sprouting regularly. Another recently announced futuristic meat replacement is named 'Air Protein' and estimates suggest that their CO_2-producing bacteria, based on NASA technology, can produce 10,000 times more food per land area and use 2000 times less water than soybeans. It's rich in vitamins and minerals and has a full complement of amino acids, making it a complete protein. It's also very concentrated, starting out with 70–80 per cent protein compared with 30–50 per cent in soy. In more good news for vegans, it contains vitamin B12.

TOBIAS LEENAERT

Tobias is a speaker and strategist. He is the author of *How to Create a Vegan World* and co-founder of food awareness organisation ProVeg.

HOW I STARTED

I first thought of quitting meat when I couldn't see any relevant moral difference that justified me petting dogs while eating cows. But because I loved eating meat so much, it was only many years later, at university, when I followed my conclusion and became vegan.

I NEVER GET OFF TRACK, EXCEPT ...

When friends offer a glass of wine or I eat bread outside of my house. I think that a little bit of flexibility makes veganism not only easier to practise but it makes it also seem easier and less strict or rigid to other people. I think that's very important.

MY THREE FAVOURITE MEALS

Moussaka, seitan bourguignon, and pumpkin lasagne.

ON COOKING

You'll need some time to get the hang of cooking without animal products. But once you have, it's so easy, natural and simple. If you're cooking for non-vegans, make sure the food is filling. If your guests leave the table hungry, they'll blame that on the fact that the food is vegan, and you don't want that.

MY IDEAL WORLD

One in which animals (and humans of course) do not suffer and are not abused or killed by humans. I'm not sure if it would be what others would call 100 per cent vegan. I think it's good to have animals in human society and to mingle. So there might be symbiotic ways for humans and animals to live together. Humans might, for example, give shelter, food, protection, medical care to a few sheep and get wool in return. But there's only a limited amount of cases that might be okay. Clean meat [grown in labs] can fit in my picture of a vegan world, provided we don't have to kill cows or use bovine growth serum.

PERFECTION

Don't try to be perfect, and remember that being a good example to others is more important and more productive than being a level-five vegan. I think we shouldn't over-focus on the details of our own consumption but give a lot more attention on how we can spread the message in the best possible way.

Clean meat

Plant-based food aside, the entire concept of killing animals for meat or growing them for eggs or dairy will soon turn on its head because we will be able to have beef without sacrificing the cow, and be able to grow milk, eggs, leather and even gelatin in laboratories, or 'breweries'. Forget breeding or growing and slaughtering an animal for one meal; in the future, a single cell from a single chicken will be able to be turned into 20 trillion chicken nuggets.

Just like we wouldn't dream of using whale oil to power our houses today, or drive a horse and buggy to the supermarket, the animal agriculture industry will likely become obsolete when clean meat and clean dairy become available to consumers. My brother, Emile Sherman, best known for his Academy Award-winning film, *The King's Speech*, was among a number of 'bold thinkers' interviewed by news site Quartz on what life in 2050 will look like. He wasn't alone in predicting the demise of meat.

'With the rise of intelligent AI, we will more and more come to appreciate the difference between intelligence and consciousness. Although animals will increasingly be recognized for their own forms of intelligence, their right to life springs from their sentience, their status as conscious creatures.

Technology will fuel this, providing us with the ability to eat meat in a way that doesn't involve taking a life, and so the preservation of conscious life will become the moral norm.[5]

Animal agriculture industries are also investing in lab-grown meats. Paul Shapiro, author of *Clean Meat*, explains: 'None of them want to be the Kodak of the meat world; everyone wants to be the Canon. Think about it: digital film displaced gelatin film and could have put both Kodak and Canon under. But Canon embraced it while Kodak resisted. We all know the end of the story: Kodak went bankrupt and Canon sells the most digital cameras today.'

Fact: **Abraham Gesner's invention of kerosene in 1849 led to the replacement of whale oil and the end of whaling in the USA.**

Most of the meat people will eat in 2040 will not come from slaughtered animals, according to a report that predicts 60 per cent will be either grown in vats or replaced by plant-based products that look and taste like meat.

One report highlights the heavy environmental impacts of conventional meat production and the concerns people have about the welfare of animals under industrial farming: 'The large-scale livestock industry is viewed by many as an unnecessary evil ... With the advantages of novel vegan meat replacements and cultured meat over conventionally produced meat, it is only a matter of time before they capture a substantial market share.'[16]

Soon we will be able to 'have our meat and eat it too'. The report estimates 35 per cent of all meat will be cultured in 2040 and 25 per cent will be vegan replacements.

'WE PLAN TO DO TO ANIMAL AGRICULTURE WHAT THE CAR DID TO THE HORSE AND BUGGY ... AFTER CLEAN MEAT IS ON THE MARKET, IT'S GOING TO BE UNIMAGINABLE THAT WE WERE OKAY WITH SLAUGHTERING BILLIONS OF ANIMALS FOR FOOD PRODUCTION DESPITE THE HARM IT WAS HAVING TO HUMAN HEALTH, THE ENVIRONMENT AND THE ECONOMIC INEFFICIENCIES.'

UMA VALETI,
MEMPHIS MEATS

My vision

I'm hardly a futurist, but I can see the tide turning and a vegan lifestyle, combined with the development of lab-grown or 'clean meat', washing us clean.

I see millions of acres of land, forests, grasslands and wetlands, currently swarming with cows and sheep, return to wild. When humans leave, nature inevitably recovers, recolonises and regenerates. Populations of flora and fauna explode, native and non-native species co-existing (as they often do). Wild grasses grow back and the soil, blossoming with fruits and flowers, will finally be unencumbered by the damage caused by the billions of cattle and sheep that once trampled upon it. Without top-soil run-off, without waste from factory farms and toxic chemicals from tanneries, rivers run fresh.

Factory farms transition from cruelty to kindness, their massive sheds no longer packed with crying creatures, but full of organic vegetables, grown with high-tech permaculture. Workers, emotionally stressed by the endless killing, are retrained into jobs where they grow and give life. Without the massive fisheries stripping our oceans and seas, marine life returns with schools of tuna, dolphins, turtles, sharks ... all thriving. Zoos, circuses and aquariums use education technology, like virtual reality, to teach our children about the natural world. Our interactions with animals are based on respect and understanding. The climate crisis has been averted and our Earth's weather patterns return to normal.

Yes, it may be a fantasy. But it certainly would be a bright future. And one I hope we will one day achieve.

YOU'VE FINISHED VEGAN LIVING, WELL DONE!

Thank you so very much for joining me on this journey through the whys, hows and whats of veganism. I sincerely appreciate your time. Finishing this book, you may feel overwhelmed with the information you've read. The damage and suffering humans are causing animals and our Earth is shocking; acquiring this knowledge is known to be traumatic for many (I know this from experience too). And what you have now learned, your new understandings, may take time to integrate into your bodies, hearts and minds and become yours, forming the new (and inevitably improved!) you. Reading this book may also have caused feelings of overwhelm at how much there is to change or adapt on the road towards a vegan lifestyle. And it's true, there's a lot to do.

But please be heartened – living a life that's full of meaning and is in line with our innermost values, our hearts, is a life that's deeply satisfying. Remember how Gandhi said, 'True happiness is when what you think, do and say are in harmony'? When we make these positive changes, rather than depleting us, they will enrich our souls and energise our bodies.

Don't forget to be kind to yourself, just as you want to be kind to other imperfect humans, other creatures, and the life-giving earth upon which we stand.

Vegan living is connected to social justice, respect, compassion but, at its very core, it's about living kindly: kindness to animals, the environment, our earth and our fellow humans. We can each play a part in spreading kindness in our daily actions and thoughts.

I hope I have shared my hope and trust that together, we can stop animal cruelty and create a healthy, kind brighter future for all beings.

Resources

This is a small selection of the many wonderful, fascinating, eye-opening books available on the subjects I've covered. Read and enjoy!

Why vegan

- *Animal Liberation*, Peter Singer
- *The Ethics of What We Eat: Why Our Food Choices Matter*, Peter Singer and Jim Mason
- *Are We Smart Enough to Know How Smart Animals Are?*, Frans de Waal
- *The Pig Who Sang to the Moon: The Emotional World of Farm Animals*, Jeffrey Moussaieff Masson
- *Eating Animals*, Jonathan Safran Foer
- *The Ten Trusts: What We Must Do to Care for the Animals We Love*, Jane Goodall and Marc Bekoff
- *The Emotional Lives of Animals*, Marc Bekoff
- *Rattling the Cage: Toward Legal Rights for Animals*, Steven M. Wise
- *Meatonomics*, David Robinson Simon
- *The Lives of Animals*, J.M. Coetzee (fiction)
- *For the Birds: From Exploitation to Liberation*, Karen Davis
- *What a Fish Knows: The Inner Lives of Our Underwater Cousins*, Jonathan Balcombe
- Voiceless legal and scientific reports on animal industries (including hens, meat chickens, pigs, dairy cows) are available for free download at www.voiceless.org.au

Health and food

- *Children's Health A to Z for New Zealand Parents,* Dr Leila Masson
- *How Not to Die: Discover the Foods Scientifically Proven to Prevent and Reverse Disease,* Dr Michael Greger, Gene Stone, et al.
- *Simple Happy Kitchen: An illustrated guide for your plant-based life,* Miki Mottes
- *Vegan for Life: Everything You Need to Know to Be Healthy and Fit on a Plant-based Diet,* Jack Norris, RD and Virginia Messina, MPH, RD
- *The Forks Over Knives Plan: How to Transition to the Life-Saving, Whole-Food, Plant-Based Diet,* Alona Pulde MD and Matthew Lederman MD

Fashion, lifestyle and advocacy

- *How to Create a Vegan World: A Pragmatic Approach,* Tobias Leenaert
- *The Animal Lover's Guide to Changing the World,* Stephanie Feldstein
- *Beasts of Burden: Animal and Disability Liberation,* Sunaura Taylor
- *Plant-Powered Women: Pioneering Female Vegan Leaders Share Their Vision for a Healthier, Greener, More Compassionate World,* Kathy Divine
- *The Sexual Politics of Meat: A Feminist-Vegetarian Critical Theory,* Carol J. Adams
- *Sistah Vegan: Black Female Vegans Speak on Food, Identity, Health and Society,* A. Breeze Harper

Your community

- 🌸 *Living Among Meat Eaters: The Vegetarian's Survival Handbook*, Carol J. Adams
- 🌸 *Why We Love Dogs, Eat Pigs and Wear Cows: An Introduction to Carnism*, Melanie Joy PhD
- 🌸 *Vystopia: The Anguish of Being Vegan in a Non-vegan World*, Clare Mann

The future

- 🌸 *Clean Meat: How Growing Meat Without Animals Will Revolutionize Dinner and the World*, Paul Shapiro

For teens

- 🌸 The Animal Allies Series (*Sky*, *Snow* and *Star*), Ondine Sherman
- 🌸 *Generation V: The Complete Guide to Going, Being, and Staying Vegan as a Teenager*, Claire Askew
- 🌸 *The Modern Day Guide to Going Vegan at a Young Age*, Avalon Llewellyn (e-book)

RECIPE BOOKS

Here are some favourites suggested by the vegan community:

- 🌸 *The Naked Vegan*, Maz Valcorza
- 🌸 *The Compassionate Kitchen*, Gemma Davis and Tracy Noelle
- 🌸 *Veganomicon: The Ultimate Vegan Cookbook*, Isa Chandra Moskowitz and Terry Hope Romero
- 🌸 *Feed Me Vegan*, Lucy Watson

- *BOSH! Healthy Vegan*, Ian Theasby and Henry David Firth
- *What Vegans Eat*, Brett Cobley
- *Isa Does It*, Isa Chandra Moskowitz
- *Epic Plant Powered Kid Food, Epic Vegan Food*, Ellen Fisher (ebooks)
- *Cooking with Kindness*, collected by Pam Ahern, Edgar's Mission
- *15 Minute Vegan* and *15 Minute Vegan on a Budget*, Katy Beskow
- *Taste for Life*, Animals Australia
- *Supermarket Vegan*, Donna Klein
- *Forks Over Knives: The Cookbook*, Del Sroufe
- *Keep it Vegan, New Vegan* and *Cook Share Eat Vegan*, Áine Carlin
- *Global Vegan*, Ellie Bullen
- *Thug Kitchen*, Thug Kitchen
- *Discovering Vegan Italian*, Nadia Fragnito
- *Vegan Cupcakes Take Over the World*, Isa Chandra Moskowitz and Terry Hope Romero
- *Deliciously Ella*, Ella Woodward
- *Thriving on Plants*, Cherie Tu
- *Vegan 100*, Gaz Oakley
- *Vegan Richa's Indian Kitchen* and *Vegan Richa's Everyday Kitchen*, Richa Hingle
- *The No Meat Athlete Cookbook*, Matt Frazier and Stepfanie Romine
- *Plant-Based on a Budget*, Toni Okamoto
- *Salad Samurai*, Terry Hope Romero
- *Vegan Planet*, Robin Robertson
- *The Great Vegan Bean Book*, Kathy Hester

- *Bake Vegan Stuff, Easy Recipes for Kids (And Adults Too!)*, Sara Kidd and Peter Chen
- *Skinny Bitch in the Kitch,* Rory Freedman and Kim Barnouin
- *The Joy of Vegan Baking,* Colleen Patrick-Goudreau

FILMS

These documentary films aim to inform, inspire, and change our hearts and minds about animals, food, society and veganism.

N.B. Check the age-rating as some can have graphic content.

- *The Game Changers* (2018)
- *Dominion* (2018)
- *73 Cows* (2018)
- *Kangaroo: A Love Hate Story* (2017)
- *The Last Pig* (2017)
- *Eating Animals* (2017)
- *The End of Meat* (2017)
- *Lucent* (2014)
- *Cowspiracy: The Sustainability Secret* (2014)
- *Live and Let Live* (2013)
- *The Ghosts in Our Machine* (2013)
- *Blackfish* (2013)
- *Vegucated* (2011)
- *Forks over Knives* (2011)
- *The Cove* (2009)
- *Food Inc.* (2008)
- *Earthlings* (2005)

APPS

If you're a smartphone addict like me, you may want to download one of these helpful apps.

- ✿ HappyCow (free, helps you find vegan-friendly food and stores around the world)
- ✿ The Darwin Challenge (free, helps you cut back on animal-products)
- ✿ Choose Cruelty Free (free, Australia based)
- ✿ Bunny Free via PETA (free, cruelty-free and vegan guide to products)
- ✿ Forks Over Knives (vegan recipes)
- ✿ Food Monster by One Green Planet (free trial, vegan recipes)
- ✿ Dr Greger's Daily Dozen (helps keep track of your servings)
- ✿ 21-Day Vegan Kickstart (meal-planning app and recipes)

Endnotes

1. THE TIME IS NOW

1   Kirby, M., 'A late-life epiphany for Michael Kirby', Sydney Morning Herald, 17 December 2011, retrieved from <https://www.smh.com.au/environment/conservation/a-late-life-epiphany-for-michael-kirby-20111217-1ozrs.html>

2   Dowding, L., The Vegan Calculator, 2019, retrieved from <https://thevegancalculator.com/#calculator>

2. WHY VEGAN

1   Dowding, L., The Vegan Calculator.

2   Edgar's Mission, About Edgar's Mission, 2019, retrieved from <https://www.edgarsmission.org.au/about-us/>

3   Voiceless, the animal protection institute, The Voiceless Animal Cruelty Index, 2019, retrieved from <https://vaci.voiceless.org.au>

4   Harari, Y.N., 'Industrial farming is one of the worst crimes in history', 2015, The Guardian, 25 September 2015, retrieved from <https://www.theguardian.com/books/2015/sep/25/industrial-farming-one-worst-crimes-history-ethical-question>

5   Jeremy Bentham, An Introduction to the Principles of Morals and Legislation (1823), reprinted by Prometheus Books, New York, 1988

6   McGreevy, P., Cornish, A. & Jones, B., 'Not just activists, 9 out of 10 people are concerned about animal welfare in Australian farming', 2019, The Conversation, 15 May 2019, retrieved from <https://theconversation.com/not-just-activists-9-out-of-10-people-are-concerned-about-animal-welfare-in-australian-farming-117077?fbclid=IwAR0Ysfu38Fm-k7TsBLgSjfl0NCkcfMkrMq--NhOeYtwgaqyhrxkMJu8p4-GU>

7   Read more about battery hens in the Voiceless report: 'Unscrambled: The hidden truth of hen welfare in the Australian egg industry', May 2017, download at <https://www.voiceless.org.au/hot-topics/battery-hens>

8   Upton Sinclair, I, Candidate for Governor: And How I Got Licked (1935), reprinted by University of California Press, 1994

9   Comis, B., The Last Pig, 7 February 2015, retrieved from <http://www.thelastpig.com/on-the-farm/>

10   Free From Harm, Dairy Farmer of 18 Years Says Cows Are Devastated When Their
      Calves Are Stolen, 5 May 2019, retrieved from <https://freefromharm.org/animal-
      farmer-turned-vegan/jackie-scurr/>

11   Voiceless the animal protection institute, 'From Paddocks to Prisons', December 2005, p.
      1, retrieved from <https://www.voiceless.org.au/hot-topics/pigs>

12   Bekoff, M., 'After 2,500 Studies, It's Time to Declare Animal Sentience Proven (Op-Ed)',
      2013, Live Science, 6 September 2013, retrieved from <https://www.livescience.
      com/39481-time-to-declare-animal-sentience.html>

13   Bekoff, M., 'Animals are conscious and should be treated as such', 19 September 2012,
      retrieved from <https://www.newscientist.com/article/mg21528836-200-animals-are-
      conscious-and-should-be-treated-as-such/>

14   McGreevy, P., Cornish, A., Jones, B., 'Not just activists, 9 out of 10 people are
      concerned about animal welfare in Australian farming', 15 May 2019, retrieved from
      <http://theconversation.com/not-just-activists-9-out-of-10-people-are-concerned-about-
      animal-welfare-in-australian-farming-117077>

15   Free From Harm, The 'Good Old Days' of Animal Farming Were Never Good for the
      Animals, 27 September 2018, retrieved from <https://freefromharm.org/animal-farmer-
      turned-vegan/matt-bear/>

16   Voiceless, the animal protection institute, The Life of the Dairy Cow: A Report on the Australian
      Dairy Industry, January 2015, p. 3, retrieved from <https://www.voiceless.org.au/sites/default/
      files/Reports/PDFS/Reports/VoicelessReport_Life_Of_The_Dairy_Cow_2013.pdf>

17   Goodall, J., 'Why I Became Vegetarian (And Why We Should All Eat Less Meat)',
      Jane Goodall's GOOD FOR ALL NEWS, 28 April 2017, retrieved from <http://news.
      janegoodall.org/2017/04/28/why-i-became-a-vegetarian-and-why-we-should-all-
      eat-less-meat/>

18   Evans, M., On Eating Meat [Kindle Edition], Murdoch Books, Australia, 1 July 2019, Loc
      117 and 139

19   Levitt, T., 'The smell, the noise, the dust: my neighbour, the factory farm', 2019,
      The Guardian, 24 July 2019, retrieved from <https://www.theguardian.com/
      environment/2019/jul/24/the-smell-the-noise-the-dust-my-neighbour-the-factory-farm?fb
      clid=IwAR2oKqbf2COsSVNuTQLpwDTVZX9TXKh9ZFTO-VjYSeTUQ9phZpiuuwsk68s>

20   An edited extract from Brian Sherman with AM Jonson, The Lives of Brian, Melbourne
      University Press, Melbourne, 2018, pp 235–37

21   Potts, A., Chicken, Reaktion Books, London, 2012, p. 46

22   Davis, K., 2009, Prisoned Chickens Poisoned Eggs: An inside look at the modern poultry
      industry, 1996, rev. K. Davis, Book Publishing Company, Summertown Tennessee, p. 10

23   Voiceless the animal protection institute, 'Unscrambled: The hidden truth of hen welfare in the Australian egg industry', May 2017, p. 7, retrieved from <https://www.voiceless.org.au/hot-topics/battery-hens>

24   Rogers, O., 'Rating Animals Quality of Life', Faunalytics, 17 May 2019, retrieved from <https://faunalytics.org/rating-animals-quality-of-life/>

25   Pickett, H., 'Industrial Animal Agriculture', Compassion in World Farming Trust, 2003, p. 2, retrieved from <https://www.ciwf.org.uk/media/3817783/industrial-animal-farming-booklet.pdf>

26   Rogers, L., The development of brain and behaviour in chicken, CABI Publishing, Wallingford, 1995, p. 219; Glatz P., Bourke, M., Barnett, J. & Critchley, K. 'Beak Trimming Training Manual' Rural Industries Research and Development Corporation (RIRDC), No. 2, February 2002, p. 1, retrieved from <https://www.australianeggs.org.au/dmsdocument/579-beak-trimming-manual>

27   Hughes, B.O. & Gentle, M.J., 'Beak trimming of poultry – its implications for welfare', World's Poultry Science Journal, Vol. 51, No. 1, 1995, pp. 51–61; Farm Animal Welfare Council (FAWC), 'Opinion on Beak Trimming of Layer Hens', November 2007, retrieved from <http://webarchive.nationalarchives.gov.uk/20121007104210/http://www.fawc.org.uk/pdf/beak-trimming.pdf>

28   Fishcount UK, 'Numbers of fish caught from wild each year', updated 2019, retrieved from <http://fishcount.org.uk/fish-count-estimates-2/numbers-of-fish-caught-from-the-wild-each-year>.

29   These pages draw upon books and articles published by fish experts including Jonathan Balcombe, Professor Culum Brown and Victoria Braithwaite. In the course of their work, these scientists have collated and reviewed hundreds of scientific papers on fish sentience, cognition and ability. Some of their research includes: Balcombe, J. What a Fish Knows, Scientific American/FSG, 2016, pp. 1–238; Brown, C., 'Fish intelligence, sentience and ethics', Animal Cognition, 2015, Vol. 18, No.1, pp. 1–17 and; Braithwaite, V., Do Fish Feel Pain?, Oxford University Press, New York, 2010, pp. 1–256.

30   Brut Media, Joaquin Phoenix tells Brut why he's vegan, 28 September 2019, retrieved from <https://www.brut.media/us/entertainment/interview-joaquin-phoenix-tells-brut-why-he-s-vegan-41090438-1fd4-4ebb-99bd-4488ebfde53c>

31   Rose, J.D., Arlinghaus, R., Cooke, S.J., Diggles, B.K., Sawynok, W., Stevens, E.D. & Wynne, C.D.L., 'Can fish really feel pain?', Fish and Fisheries, Vol. 15, No. 1, pp. 97–133, 2012, retrieved from <https://doi.org/10.1111/faf.12010>

32   Low, P., 'The Cambridge Declaration on Consciousness', in Francis Crick Memorial Conference, Cambridge, England, 7 July 2012

33   Broom, D.M., Sentience and Animal Welfare, CABI, Wallingford, 2014, p. 61

34   Wong, K. 'Brainy Bees Think Abstractly', Scientific American, 23 April 2001, retrieved from <https://www.scientificamerican.com/article/brainy-bees-think-abstrac/>

35   Hurst, E., Inaugural Speech to the NSW Legislative Council Hansard, transcript, 29 May 2019, retrieved from <https://www.parliament.nsw.gov.au/member/files/2254/Hon%20 Emma%20Hurst%20-%20Inaugural%20speech.pdf>

36   Read more about dairy cows in the Voiceless Report: 'The Life of the Dairy Cow: A Report on the Australian Dairy Industry', January 2015, found at <https://www.voiceless.org.au/sites/ default/files/Reports/PDFS/Reports/VoicelessReport_Life_Of_The_Dairy_Cow_2013.pdf>

37

38

Voiceless, the animal protection institute, 'The Life of the Dairy Cow: A Report on the Australian Dairy Industry', January 2015, p. 4, retrieved from <https://www.voiceless.org.au/sites/ default/files/Reports/PDFS/Reports/VoicelessReport_Life_Of_The_Dairy_Cow_2013.pdf>

Free From Harm, 'Dairy Farmer of 18 Years Says Cows Are Devastated When Calves Are Stolen', 5 May 2019, retrieved from <https://freefromharm.org/animal-farmer-turned-vegan/jackie-scurr/>

39   Intergovernmental Panel on Climate Change, Climate Change 2014 Synthesis Report Summary for Policymakers, 2014, retrieved from <https://www.ipcc.ch/site/assets/ uploads/2018/02/AR5_SYR_FINAL_SPM.pdf>

40   Koneswaran, G., and Nierenberg, D., 'Global Farm Animal Production and Global Warming: Impacting and Mitigating Climate Change', Environmental Health Perspectives, 2008, Vol. 116, No. 5, 578–82, doi: 10.1289/ehp.11034

41   Chiorando, M., 'Leonardo DiCaprio Brands Vegan Meat "The Future"', Plant Based News, 28 September 2018, retrieved from <https://www.plantbasednews.org/news/ leonardo-dicaprio-vegan-meat-future>

42   Page, T., 'The beef with beef', CNN Health, 12 December 2018, retrieved from <https:// edition.cnn.com/2018/12/11/health/the-beef-with-beef/index.html>

43   Carrington, D., 'Giving up beef will reduce carbon footprint more than cars, says expert', The Guardian, 22 July 2014, retrieved from <https://www.theguardian.com/ environment/2014/jul/21/giving-up-beef-reduce-carbon-footprint-more-than-cars>

44   Steinfeld, H., Gerber, P., Wassenaar, T.D., Castel, V., Rosales, M., Rosales, M. and de Haan, C., Livestock's long shadow: environmental issues and options, Food & Agriculture Organization of the United Nations, 2006, p. iii, retrieved from <http://www.fao.org/3/ a0701e/a0701e00.htm>

45   Foer, J.S., 'Jonathan Safran Foer: why we must cut out meat and dairy before dinner to save the planet', The Guardian, 28 September 2019, retrieved from <https://www.

theguardian.com/books/2019/sep/28/meat-of-the-matter-the-inconvenient-truth-about-what-we-eat?CMP=Share_iOSApp_Other>

46   Bold Vegan, 'The Periodic Table of Vegan and Vegetarian Stars', Visually, 21 Nov 2012, retrieved from <https://visual.ly/community/infographic/food/periodic-table-vegan-and-vegetarian-stars>

47   Xavantina, N. and Santarém, 'The Amazon is approaching an irreversible tipping point', The Economist, 1 August 2019, retrieved from <https://www.economist.com/briefing/2019/08/01/the-amazon-is-approaching-an-irreversible-tipping-point>

48   Mackintosh, E., 'The Amazon is burning because the world eats so much meat', CNN World, 23 August 2019, retrieved from <https://edition.cnn.com/2019/08/23/americas/brazil-beef-amazon-rainforest-fire-intl/index.html>

49   'Soy Agriculture in the Amazon Basin', Global Forest Atlas, 2019 <https://globalforestatlas.yale.edu/amazon/land-use/soy>

50   Food and Agriculture Organization of the United Nations, 'Livestock a major threat to environment, Remedies urgently needed', FAO Newsroom, 26 November 2006, retrieved from <http://www.fao.org/newsroom/en/news/2006/1000448/index.html>

51   Ceballos, G., Ehrlich, P.R, and Dirzo, R., 'Biological annihilation via the ongoing sixth mass extinction signalled by vertebrate population losses and declines', Proceedings of the National Academy of Sciences of the United States of America, 2017, Vol. 144, No. 30, pp. E6080-E6096, retrieved from <https://doi.org/10.1073/pnas.1704949114>

52   Díaz, S., Settele, J., Brondízio, E., et al., Summary for policymakers of the global assessment report on biodiversity and ecosystem services of the Intergovernmental Science-Policy Platform on Biodiversity and Ecosystem Services – Advanced Unedited Version, 6 May 2019, p. 3, retrieved from <https://www.ipbes.net/sites/default/files/downloads/spm_unedited_advance_for_posting_htn.pdf>

53   Bold Vegan, 'The Periodic Table of Vegan and Vegetarian Stars', Visually, 21 Nov 2012, retrieved from <https://visual.ly/community/infographic/food/periodic-table-vegan-and-vegetarian-stars>

54   UN Water, Water, Food and Energy, retrieved from <http://www.unwater.org/water-facts/water-food-and-energy/>

55   Food and Agriculture Organization of the United Nations, 'Livestock a major threat to environment, Remedies urgently needed', FAO Newsroom, 26 November 2006, retrieved from <http://www.fao.org/newsroom/en/news/2006/1000448/index.html>

56   Attenborough, D. 'David Attenborough: "The Garden of Eden is no more". Read his Davos speech in full', World Economic Forum, 21 January 2019, retrieved from <https://www.weforum.org/agenda/2019/01/david-attenborough-transcript-from-crystal-

award-speech/>

3. HEALTH & FOOD

1   Harvard Women's Health Watch, 'Becoming a vegetarian', Harvard Health Publishing, 23 October 2018, retrieved from <https://www.health.harvard.edu/staying-healthy/becoming-a-vegetarian>

2   Brody, J.E., 'Huge Study of Diet Indicts Fat and Meat', The New York Times, 8 May 1990, retrieved from <https://www.nytimes.com/1990/05/08/science/huge-study-of-diet-indicts-fat-and-meat.html>

3   Haelle, T., '10 Nutrition Studies Funded by Big Business', Everyday Health, 6 October 2015, retrieved from <https://www.everydayhealth.com/pictures/nutrition-studies-funded-big-business/>

4   Lanou, A.J., and Svenson, B., 'Reduced cancer risk in vegetarians: an analysis of recent reports', Cancer Management and Research, 2010, Vol. 3, pp. 1–8, doi: 10.2147/CMR.S6910

5   Nestle, M. 'Industry-funded study of the week: Dairy yet again', Food Politics, 21 October 2019, retrieved from <https://www.foodpolitics.com/2019/10/industry-funded-study-of-the-week-dairy-yet-again/>

6   Newman, T., 'Vegetarian diet reduces heart disease death risk by 40 percent', Medical News Today, 1 June 2018, retrieved from <https://www.medicalnewstoday.com/articles/321992.php>

7   Turner-McGrievy, G., Mandes, T., & Crimarco, A., 'A plant-based diet for overweight and obesity prevention and treatment', Journal of Geriatric Cardiology, 2017, Vol. 14, No. 5, pp. 369–74, doi: 10.11909/j.issn.1671-5411.2017.05.002

8   Waddell, J., 'But You Kill Ants, Answers to 101 concerns about vegetarianism and veganism', Vegan Australia, 2013, retrieved from <https://www.veganaustralia.org.au/but_you_kill_ants>

9   Elliot, R., 'Donald Watson, the first vegan, who invented the word – and outlived his many critics', The Guardian, 14 January 2006, retrieved from <https://www.theguardian.com/news/2006/jan/14/guardianobituaries.food>

10 Voiceless, the animal protection institute, The Voiceless Animal Cruelty Index (VACI), 2019, retrieved from <https://vaci.voiceless.org.au>

11 McFarlane, G., response to survey from author: 'New Vegan Guidebook – your advice needed [...]', SurveyMonkey Inc., 6 July 2019, San Mateo, California, USA, www.surveymonkey.com

12   Hobbs, M., response to survey from author: 'New Vegan Guidebook – your advice needed […]', SurveyMonkey Inc., 9 November 2019, San Mateo, California, USA, www.surveymonkey.com

13   Yale Environment 360, 'Food Industry Pursues the Strategy of Big Tobacco', Yale Environment 360, 8 April 2009, retrieved from <https://e360.yale.edu/features/food_industry_pursues_the_strategy_of_big_tobacco>

14   Edsor, B., 'These 14 elite athletes are vegan – here's what made them switch their diet', Insider, 1 November 2017, retrieved from <https://www.insider.com/elite-athletes-who-are-vegan-and-what-made-them-switch-their-diet-2017-10>

15   Fasanella, K., 'Professional Surfer Tia Blanco Talks Sexism, Body Image, and Vegan Favorites', Teen Vogue, 28 July 2017, retrieved from <https://www.teenvogue.com/story/professional-surfer-tia-blanco-body-image-vegan>

16   Smith, K., 'All The 'Smart' Athletes Are Going Vegan, Says NBA Star John Salley', Live Kindly, 6 June 2019, retrieved from <https://www.livekindly.co/smart-athletes-going-vegan-nba-star-john-salley/>

17   Divine, K., response to survey by author: 'New Vegan Guidebook – your advice needed […] SurveyMonkey Inc., 6 July 2019, San Mateo, California, USA, www.surveymonkey.com

18   Mottes, M., Simple Happy Kitchen- An Illustrated Guide for Your Plant-Based Life, Simple Happy Kitchen, 2018, p. 51

19   Pendick, D., 'How much protein do you need every day?', Harvard Health Publishing, 18 June 2015, retrieved from <https://www.health.harvard.edu/blog/how-much-protein-do-you-need-every-day-201506188096>

20   Marsh, K.A., Munn, E.A., and Baines, S.K., 'Protein and vegetarian diets', The Medical Journal of Australia, 2013, Vol. 199, No. 4, pp. S7–S10, retrieved from <https://www.ncbi.nlm.nih.gov/pubmed/25369930>

21   'Vegans may lack essential nutrient intake, study reports', Science Daily, 16 March 2016, retrieved from <https://www.sciencedaily.com/releases/2016/03/160316194551.htm>

22   Videle, J., 'Comparison of Protein and Caloric Energy (KCal) Produced Per Acre on U.S. Farms', Humane Herald, 9 May 2019, retrieved from <https://humaneherald.org/2019/05/09/comparison-of-protein-and-caloric-energy-kcal-produced-per-acre-on-u-s-farms/>

23   Arnarson, A., 'Does Dairy Cause or Prevent Cancer? An Objective Look', Healthline, 4 June 2017, retrieved from <https://www.healthline.com/nutrition/dairy-and-cancer>

24   UCSF Health, Calcium Content of Foods, retrieved from <https://www.ucsfhealth.org/education/calcium_content_of_selected_foods/>

25   Craig, W.J., Mangels, A.R. and American Dietetic Association, 'Position of the American Dietetic Association: vegetarian diets', Journal of the American Dietetic Association, 2009, Vol. 109, No. 7, pp. 1266-82, doi: 10.1016/j.jada.2009.05.027

26   Brody, J.E., 'Huge Study of Diet Indicts Fat and Meat', The New York Times, 8 May 1990, retrieved from <https://www.nytimes.com/1990/05/08/science/huge-study-of-diet-indicts-fat-and-meat.html>

27   Hobbs, M., response to survey from author: 'New Vegan Guidebook – your advice needed […] SurveyMonkey Inc., 6 July 2019, San Mateo, California, USA, www.surveymonkey.com

28   Physicians Committee for Responsible Medicine, Soy and Health, 2018, retrieved from <https://www.pcrm.org/good-nutrition/nutrition-information/soy-and-health>

29   Groves, M., 'Is Soy Good or Bad for Your Health?', Healthline, 22 November 2018, retrieved from <https://www.healthline.com/nutrition/soy-good-or-bad#downsides>

30   Rowland, M.P., 'This Is Your Brain On Cheese, Forbes, 26 June 2017, retrieved from <https://www.forbes.com/sites/michaelpellmanrowland/2017/06/26/cheese-addiction/#2447ba433583>

31   Kruse, R.W., and Dubowy, S.M., 'Calcium', Kids Health, 2017, retrieved from <https://kidshealth.org/en/parents/calcium.html>

32   Mayo Clinic, Pregnancy week by week, 2017, retrieved from <https://www.mayoclinic.org/healthy-lifestyle/pregnancy-week-by-week/in-depth/pregnancy-nutrition/art-20045082>

33   Physicians Committee for Responsible Medicine, A Natural Approach to Menopause, retrieved from <https://www.pcrm.org/good-nutrition/nutrition-information/a-natural-approach-to-menopause>

34   Groves, M., 'Menopause Diet: How What You Eat Affects Your Symptoms, Healthline, 23 November 2018, <https://www.healthline.com/nutrition/menopause-diet#foods-to-eat>

35   Physicians Committee for Responsible Medicine, Preventing and Reversing Osteoporosis, retrieved from <https://www.pcrm.org/good-nutrition/nutrition-information/health-concerns-about-dairy/preventing-and-reversing-osteoporosis>

4. FASHION LIFESTYLE & ADVOCACY

1   Anna Starostinetskaya, 'Beastie Boys Partner with Adidas to Launch Vegan Shoe', VegNews, 26 July 2019, retrieved from <https://vegnews.com/2019/7/beastie-boys-

partner-with-adidas-to-launch-vegan-shoe>

2   Interviewee Isogawa, Akira. Personal interview by Jonson, A., and Sherman B., Skype, 11 September 2019.

3   O'Connell, L., 'Leather goods market value forecast worldwide from 2016 until 2021 (in billion US dollars)*', Statista, 15 November 2018, retrieved from <https://www.statista.com/statistics/861562/leather-goods-market-value-worldwide/>

4   Grosso, M., Amazon Cattle Footprint: The State of Destruction, Greenpeace, 2009, retrieved from <https://www.greenpeace.org/usa/wp-content/uploads/legacy/Global/usa/report/2010/2/amazon-cattle-footprint.pdf>

5   Biello D., 'World's 10 Worst Toxic Pollution Problems [Slide Show]', Scientific American, 10 November 2011, retrieved from <https://www.scientificamerican.com/article/10-worst-toxic-pollution-problems-slide-show/>

6   European Food Safety Authority (EFSA), 'Scientific Opinion on the welfare of cattle kept for beef production and the welfare in intensive calf farming systems', EFSA Journal, 2012, Vol. 10, No. 5, pp. 1–166, doi: 10.2903/j.efsa.2012.2669

7   'Fast Fashion Is a Disaster for Women and The Environment', Forbes, 26 July 2017, retrieved from <https://www.forbes.com/sites/quora/2017/07/26/fast-fashion-is-a-disaster-for-women-and-the-environment/#422008e31fa4>

8   Read more about kangaroo killing at https://www.voiceless.org.au/hot-topics/kangaroos

9   Commonwealth of Australia, 'National Code of Practice for the Humane Shooting of Kangaroos and Wallabies for Commercial Purposes', 2008, retrieved from <https://www.environment.gov.au/system/files/resources/8ae26c87-fb7c-4ddc-b5df-02039cf1483e/files/code-conduct-commercial.pdf>

10   Voiceless, the animal protection institute, Kangaroos, July 2019, retrieved from <https://www.voiceless.org.au/hot-topics/kangaroos>

11   Nicholls, D., 'The Kangaroo – Falsely Maligned by Tradition', in Wilson, M., and Croft, D.B., Kangaroos: Myths and Realities, The Australian Wildlife Protection Council Inc., 3rd ed, 2005, pp. 33–41

12   The Law Society of NSW, Ban on the Importation of Certain Fur Products, 2019, retrieved from <https://www.lawsociety.com.au/legal-communities/NSW-young-lawyers/committees/animal-law/fur>

13   Marino, L. and Merskin, D., 'Intelligence, complexity, and individuality in sheep', Animal Sentience, pp. 206, 2019, retrieved from <https://animalstudiesrepository.org/cgi/viewcontent.cgi?article=1374&context=animsent>

14   Edwards, L.E., 'Lamb mulesing: impact on welfare and alternative', CAB Reviews, 2012, Vol. 7, No. 61, pp. 1–7, doi: 10.1079/PAVSNNR20127061

15   Wahlquist, C., 'Five ways to make horse racing more humane right now', The Guardian, 4 November 2019, retrieved from <https://www.theguardian.com/sport/2019/nov/04/five-ways-to-make-horse-racing-more-humane-right-now>

16   http://leginfo.legislature.ca.gov/faces/billTextClient.xhtml?bill_id=201920200SB313

17   Díaz, G., 'Answers: Raw Food for Cats, What About Eating Bones?', Feline Nutrition Foundation, 9 March 2019, retrieved from <https://feline-nutrition.org/answers/answers-raw-diets-and-cats-what-about-eating-bones>

18   Nicholas Coady, Suffering by Design – Why We Need Better Laws to Regulate Designer Dog Breeding, Voiceless blog, 16 September 2019, retrieved from <https://www.voiceless.org.au/content/suffering-by-design>

19   Ellis, E.G., 'Is it OK to Make Your Dog Vegan?', WIRED, 4 May 2019, retrieved from <https://www.wired.com/story/is-it-ok-to-make-your-dog-vegan/>

20   Marsh, J., and Suttie, J., 'Is a Happy Life Different from a Meaningful One?', Greater Good Magazine, 25 February, retrieved from <https://greatergood.berkeley.edu/article/item/happy_life_different_from_meaningful_life>

21   Interviewee Isogawa, Akira. Personal interview by Jonson, A., and Sherman B., by Skype, 11 September 2019

22   Pevreall, K., 'Black Veganism Rooted in Social Justice, Activists Tell New York Times', Livekindly, retrieved from <https://www.livekindly.co/black-veganism-social-justice/>

23   Carol J. Adams, Examples of Sexual Politics of Meat, 2018, retrieved from <https://caroljadams.com/examples-of-spom>

24   Chiorando, M., 'Natalie Portman Gives Pro-Vegan Speech To 16,000 Students', Plant Based News, 26 April 2019, retrieved from <https://www.plantbasednews.org/news/natalie-portman-pro-vegan-speech-16-000-students>

5. YOUR COMMUNITY

1   Grassian, T., Meat Reduction & Vegan Promotion Summary Report: Motivators, barriers, and dietary changes from the largest study of participants in meat reduction & vegan campaigns, 25 March 2019, <https://forusallsite.files.wordpress.com/2019/03/grassian-reductionandveganpromotion-v2.pdf>

2   Faunalytics, 'A Summary of Faunalytics' Study of Current and Former Vegetarians and Vegans', Faunalytics, 24 February 2016, retrieved from <https://faunalytics.org/a-summary-of-faunalytics-study-of-current-and-former-vegetarians-and-vegans/>

3   Lockwood, A., 'Do 84% Of Vegans And Vegetarians Really Go Back To Eating Meat?', Plant Based News, 7 January 2019, retrieved from <https://www.plantbasednews.org/post/do-84-

vegans-and-vegetarians-give-up-diets>

4   Mann, C., Vystopia: the anguish of being vegan in a non-vegan world, 2019, retrieved from
     <https://vystopia.com/>

5   Cole, M., and Morgan, K., 'Vegaphobia: derogatory discourses of veganism and the
     reproduction of speciesism in UK national newspapers', The British Journal of Sociology,
     2011, Vol. 62, No. 1, pp. 134–53, doi:10.1111/j.1468-4446.2010.01348.x

6   Joy, M., Why We Love Dogs, Eat Pigs and Wear Cows: An Introduction to Carnism,
     Conari Press, USA, 2009, pp. 96–97

7   Minson, J.A., and Monin, B., 'Do-Gooder Derogation: Disparaging Morally Motivated
     Minorities To Defuse Anticipated Reproach', SAGE Journals, 2011, Vol. 3, No. 2, pp.
     200–07, https://doi.org/10.1177/1948550611415695

8   Joy, M., Beyond Beliefs: A Guide to Improving Relationships and Communication for
     Vegans, Vegetarians, and Meat Eaters, Lantern Books, New York, 2018, p. 63

9   Klein, E., 'There's no conflict between human and animal rights', Vox, 21 August 2019,
     retrieved from <https://www.vox.com/future-perfect/2019/8/21/20812623/animal-
     rights-suffering-singer-compassion>

10   Vegan Neuropsychologist, 'When we care about one social justice [...]', Facebook
     post, 12 July 2018, viewed 12 July 2018, retrieved from <https://www.facebook.com/
     permalink.php?id=1851283448447286&story_fbid=2113486315560330>

11   Chiorando, M., 'Environmentalist Greta Thunberg Made Her Parents Feel Guilty For
     Eating Meat And Dairy', Plant Based News, 29 April 2019, retrieved from <https://www.
     plantbasednews.org/news/vegan-greta-thunberg-made-parents-feel-guilty-eating-
     meat-dairy>

12   Kim, S., 'Our Brains Are Wired For Empathy', Brain World Magazine, 27 June 2019,
     retrieved from <https://brainworldmagazine.com/brains-wired-empathy/>

6. THE FUTURE

1   Tubb, C., and Seba, T., Rethinking Food and Agriculture 2020-2030: The Second
     Domestication of Plants and Animals, the Disruption of the Cow, and the Collapse of
     Industrial Livestock Farming, RethinkX, September 2019, retrieved from <https://static1.
     squarespace.com/static/585c3439be65942f022bbf9b/t/5d7fe0e83d119516bfc001
     7e/1568661791363/RethinkX+Food+and+Agriculture+Report.pdf>

2   Spingmann, M., Clark, M., Mason-D'Croz, D., Wiebe, K. Bodirsky, B.L., Lassaletta,
     L., de Vries, W., Vermeulen, S.J., Herrero, M., Carlson, K.M., Jonell, M., Troell, M.,
     DeClerck, F., Gordon, L.J., Zurayk, R., Scarborough, P., Rayner, M., Loken, B., Fanzo, J.,

Godfray, H.C.J., Tilman, D., Rockström, J., & Willett, W., 'Options for keeping the food system within environmental limits', Nature, 2018, Vol. 562, pp. 519–27 doi: 10.1038/s41586-018-0594-0

3   Tubb, C., and Seba, T., Rethinking Food and Agriculture 2020-2030: The Second Domestication of Plants and Animals, the Disruption of the Cow, and the Collapse of Industrial Livestock Farming, RethinkX, September 2019, retrieved from <https://static1.squarespace.com/static/585c3439be65942f022bbf9b/t/5d7fe0e83d119516bfc0017e/1568661791363/RethinkX+Food+and+Agriculture+Report.pdf>

4   Miley, J., 'Richard Branson Thinks, By 2050, We Will No Longer Need to Kill Any Animals for Meat', Interesting Engineering, 2 October 2017, retrieved from <https://interestingengineering.com/richard-branson-thinks-by-2050-we-will-no-longer-need-to-kill-any-animals-for-meat>

5   Sherman, E., 'We asked some of the boldest thinkers what the world will be like in 50 years. Here's what their answers tell us about the future', Quartz, 2019, retrieved from <https://qz.com/is/the-world-in-50-years/expert/1708193/>

6   Gerhardy, C., Suhlmann, G., Ziemßen, F., Donnan, D., Warschun, M., and Kühnle, H.J., 'How Will Cultured Meat and Meat Alternatives Disrupt the Agricultural and Food Industry', ATKearney, retrieved from <https://www.atkearney.com/retail/article/?/a/how-will-cultured-meat-and-meat-alternatives-disrupt-the-agricultural-and-food-industry>

Acknowledgements

Huge thanks to Marty Green and Ali Green and their wonderful team at Pantera Press, including Anne, Anna and Lex, for supporting me and this book. Dr Leila Masson was so generous with her time and sharing her professional expertise. I want to acknowledge the many people who lived vegan lifestyles for decades, way before it became well known, and who are the real trailblazers to this wonderful life. Thank you to the 150 vegans for sharing their tips, tricks, thoughts and feelings via my online survey. Many other friends and colleagues contributed via lengthy interviews and quotes, big thanks to each and every one of you. Thank you also to the Hon. Emma Hurst for allowing me to publish your powerful speech. My Voiceless team, past and present, is just awesome – thanks particularly to Dr Meg Good and Ashleigh Rumpler for their input and help with this project. I'm lucky enough to have a large family and family-in-law of smart, thoughtful individuals who are all powerhouses in their own right. My daughter, Jasmine, gave insightful comments; my husband, Dror, is my rock; and my mum, Gene, a tireless cheering-squad. My dad, Brian, has been my partner in Voiceless since the start and I'm infinitely grateful for every moment we've had working together. Emile, I loved your future vision – go vegan, you can do it! My sweet boys, Dov and Lev, I can't write an acknowledgement without saying how much I love you. Since this book is a partly an ode to animals – a shout-out to my dogs, Ketem (a senior citizen who lies next to me 24/7), Nelson (the sweetest rescue dog ever) and my band of furry street cats and adopted chickens and bunnies. You all keep me sane.

Ondine Sherman is the co-founder and managing director of Voiceless, the animal protection institute. She is a life-long animal advocate, passionate about promoting respect and compassion for all creatures. Ondine holds a BA in Communications and MA in Environmental Studies. She is an ambassador for Action for Dolphins and director of conservation NGO This is My Earth (TiME), and writes regularly about animal protection in the media.

The Animal Allies series is Ondine's fiction series aimed at middle-grade readers, and *Vegan Living* is her first non-fiction book.

Ondine grew up in Sydney and now lives in Tel Aviv with her husband and three children. Her mischievous street cats, loyal dogs and ex-battery chickens all keep her extraordinarily entertained.

Looking for ways to
reduce your impact?

Check out
another great
read from
Lost the Plot

"Ways to live that favour our health, happiness,
land & oceans. I can't recommend
this book highly enough."
- ELYSE KNOWLES

I
QUIT
PLASTICS
and you can too

60+ lifestyle recipes to cut waste,
live clean and change the world

KATE NELSON